Advent Unhurried

Advent Unhurried

DAILY DEVOTIONS for a SEASON of WONDER and STILLNESS

Micha Boyett

BrazosPress
a division of Baker Publishing Group
Grand Rapids, Michigan

Published by Brazos Press
a division of Baker Publishing Group
Grand Rapids, Michigan
BrazosPress.com

Printed in the United States of America

Library of Congress Cataloging-in-Publication Data

Names: Boyett, Micha author
Title: Advent unhurried : daily devotions for a season of wonder and stillness / by Micha Boyett.
Description: Grand Rapids, Michigan : Brazos Press, a division of Baker Publishing Group, [2026]
Identifiers: LCCN 2026015454 | ISBN 9781587436109 cloth | ISBN 9781493456420 ebook
Subjects: LCSH: Advent | LCGFT: Devotional literature | Prayers
Classification: LCC BV40 .B688 2026
LC record available at https://lccn.loc.gov/2026015454

Micha Boyett is represented by the literary offices of The Zoë Pagnamenta Agency.

Baker Publishing Group publications use paper produced from sustainable forestry practices and postconsumer waste whenever possible.

26 27 28 29 30 31 32 7 6 5 4 3 2 1

For Mom,

who modeled prayer every morning of my growing up.
I pray because you taught me how.

*

CONTENTS

Note from the Author

This book contains short essays, poems, and prayer practices. The poems "Bearing Peace" and "Motherhood" were both originally commissioned in 2010 by John Knox Presbyterian Church in Seattle, Washington, and titled "The Lord Is With Thee" and "Darkness." They have both been revised from their original form. The poem "Pockets" was previously published as a digital feature for Inkwell's Winter Collection, 2026, and is published here with permission. "Joy" was featured in *Re:Echo Journal* through the generosity of Brazos Press.

Additionally, some of the essays and prayer practices were revised from original essays I posted on my Substack newsletter, *The Slow Way*.

Introduction

Slowing Down to Savor the Mystery

I am a big fan of Mary—as in the mother of God. I'm not unique. After all, much of this world is devoted to Mary, whether their devotion is an admiration or a full-fledged rosary habit. For this Protestant ex-evangelical from Texas, my attachment to the mother of Jesus began the first time I dressed as her and held a baby doll for the church photographer in my preschool Sunday school class. I was a little girl with a longing to serve God in a Southern Baptist church, where women's roles in leadership were relegated to the nurture of children, the teaching of other women, and the support of husbands. I wanted to pass the offering plate, pray the prayers everyone else bowed their heads to. I wanted to preach. I didn't know how to reconcile that longing with our church's sanctuary of stained-glass images of men. But December would arrive, and suddenly Mary, who never graced a stained-glass window in my church, appeared in our stories, songs, and prayers. Once a year, we read her poem of worship, her call for a rebalance of power. Every Christmas, she was the focus of our shared story: nurturing and faithful, a subversive saint with the voice of a poet. She was mine.

Mary's posture of courage, consent, and slow transformation has rightfully driven the story of Christ's birth for two millennia as Christians have told and retold the narrative. Mary said yes to an invitation that changed her and the world. And, like Mary, we are invited in this season to practice giving our consent to the Spirit of God, even when it means risking everything. This book invites us to slow down enough to notice God at work in and around us and, like Mary, choose to live in the mystery.

What are you invited to say yes to this Advent? Perhaps you picked up this book because you saw that word *unhurried* in the title and thought, *That's what I want*. If so, here's some good news and bad news: Good news? The weeks leading up to Christmas can be meaningful, generous, and nonanxious. The bad news? I'm no life-edit expert or self-help guru. I'm not here with a new system for organization or a plan to streamline your December. But I can offer you a rhythm to return to each day this Advent. I can offer you practices that make space to pay attention to the wonder beneath the external expectations of the season. Usually what we need more than a life hack is spaciousness, the time and intentionality to breathe and reflect.

We all long to make this season meaningful, to find some way to push back on the most chronically chaotic few weeks of the year. How can we remember who we are and who God is when our days are spent frantically shopping, baking cookies, attending parties, and sitting through the kids' performances? And, perhaps most important, who do we want to be when Christmas Day arrives?

As Annie Dillard so wisely said, "How we spend our days is, of course, how we spend our lives."[1] An unhurried Advent doesn't demand that we drop the baking, shopping, or performance attending. What matters is the posture of our souls. We can move through the demanding expectations of the season with a peaceful presence or with a frenetic energy. And what we choose will determine who we are when we finally join the people we love around the tree in four weeks.

This book is an opportunity to bring the story of Christmas into your daily rhythm this December. It's a gentle nudge to slow down enough not only to reflect on the cosmic event of Christmas but also to invite that story to affect the way you spend time with the people you love, how you play and work and rest for the next four weeks. Engaging with the story of Christ's birth begins with slowing down enough to notice it.

Years ago, the Christian contemplative Ruth Haley Barton wrote of an encounter with a spiritual director who said to her, "Ruth, you are like a jar of river water all shaken up. What you need is to sit still long enough so that the sediment can settle and the water can become clear."[2] While the chaos of this season may leave us feeling murky, our inner selves don't have to accept the unsettled state of our souls. It takes only a bit of silence and stillness to clarify the sediment of our overworked and overfilled days. We need space for God to do good work inside us, and when we create room to quiet our bodies and minds, our souls quiet down right along with them.

For most of us, the weeks before Christmas mirror the culture's wider notion of the "holiday season." But originally, Advent was woven into the church calendar as a season of reflection and fasting, preparing the way for Christmas. We may be buying gifts, singing the songs of the season, stringing lights, and stretching the celebration as long as possible before December 25, but when Advent first took shape, it was meant to be a quiet season, a season of self-exploration and amend-making. Christmas Day and the eleven days that followed were intended to be the actual time of celebration.

We don't live in a world where we can spend the four weeks leading up to Christmas tinsel-free. But we can make choices that slow us down enough to get at the intention behind Advent's early vision of preparation. How do we move out of the chaos of pre-Christmas and into a posture that embraces transformation?

Like Barton's story of river water, our time together in this book is an experiment in sitting still long enough for the sediment of our souls to settle. When our priority of the season is tending our interior lives in preparation for Christmas, the rest of the month's obligations might just sink into second place. We can't remove the expectation to party hop, bargain hunt, and regularly schlepp bags of gifts and stacks of cards from place to place, but we can reorder what matters in this season. We can say no to the invitations that don't serve our souls. We can choose to make this season one of preparation, even in the midst of chaos.

An unhurried Advent begins with letting the story of Christmas come to life. That cast of nativity characters paused in reverence on your mantel is an invitation to a far-fetched, fantastical story that claims to have changed the world. We're going to sit with their stories: parents bewildered by the presence of a baby they didn't ask for (and trying their best), the angels and the shepherds, the wise kings following a star, the older cousin also miraculously pregnant, the midwife who is never mentioned, the owners of the feeding trough and animals. These were people as hounded by confusion, limitations, and longings as the rest of us. And, perhaps, each of them wanted to believe just as much as you do, no matter how mysterious it all seems.

This is a remarkable story made even more worthy due to its peculiarity. Of course, we who have encountered this wild tale every December may forget that it is very strange: a pregnant virgin, her child from God, the angels breaking into song in the night sky over a tiny town. But its oddness is subversive. We love it because the story's strangeness is sacred. It's a story worth telling again and again, worthy of its own songs and pageants playacted by kindergarteners in robes. This is a story that sparks our inner longings for wonder and goodness and divine love. If we want to engage the Christmas story in an unhurried, contemplative way, paying attention to the experiences that settle the sediment of our jar, let's start with the most surprising hero of the tale. Mary, an unlikely girl from a town in the middle of nowhere, who says yes, accepts an invitation to leap toward a calling so nonsensical and unreasonable it could only come from God.

This Advent, we can also take a leap toward the nonsensical goodness of God. For the next four weeks, we'll be exploring four themes of the season that have the potential to reshape us and the spaces we inhabit: *hope*, *peace*, *joy*, and *love*. We return to these virtues every Advent as we light the candles on our tables and in our churches. While we sometimes talk of virtues as rules we should follow, something we should add to our list of self-improvement tasks, Aristotle didn't see virtues that way. The father of virtue ethics, Aristotle understood a moral virtue as an interior habit cultivated over time, which eventually shapes our actions.[3] He believed that once these virtues become part of us through intentional formation, we will reliably choose what is good for us and the people around us in high-stakes moments. So virtues are not something we apply in critical situations, simply because we've been taught right from wrong; instead, virtues are built in us over time, training our brains so that we will make wise choices for ourselves and our communities. In other words, Aristotle tells us, "We become just by doing just acts, temperate by doing temperate acts, brave by doing brave acts."[4]

We can think of this habit building as "practice," a word we often use in spiritual conversations. Just as an athlete practices their skill until it is second nature, we practice the virtues we long to embody. Author Mark Scandrette calls this kind of practice taking a new posture, integrating these virtues by engaging our bodies, so that our actions reflect our inner experience.[5] To embrace a virtue in this way is not simply to accept the idea of it but to let that concept transform our orientation to the world. In this way, a virtue is far more than a thought exercise; it's a way of being that results in actions that reflect the good we've allowed to grow within us. Hope, peace, joy, and love help us not just access this story of the birth of Jesus; they become part of who we are, awake to all God is up to in the world.

Like Mary, we are being offered a wild and dangerous calling this season—to be bearers of transformation, people who orient our lives around hope, peace, joy, and love. In the midst of being misunderstood and most likely rejected by her community, Mary managed to hold on to the promise God gave her. How did she embrace a story so mysterious and impossible to believe? She did what all of us are invited to do: make use of our sacred imagination. When I use the phrase "sacred imagination," I'm referring to our inner creativity that allows us to reconceive the world, dreaming of a reality more beautiful and true than we currently experience. This is not imagination as we usually think of it, as in fiction and fairy tales; it's the inner work of allowing the good gifts of life to awaken our perspectives, our longing for peace and joy and hope to guide us into a richer life.

This may surprise you, but we already know how to do this! Each December when we string twinkle lights, sing songs, dress up for parties, and tip back our sparkly drinks, we are playfully envisioning the divine. To engage with the wonder of Christmas through our imaginations is to practice belief, even if that just means putting ourselves in Mary's position as we sing a Christmas hymn, or decorating our mantle with candles, our own version of angelic fireworks above the manger. We start with the ancient story, but we live it in our present day, as we reflect on the mystery and then allow it to transform who we are and how we live in the world. Using our sacred imagination is its own form of prayer, a way of creatively stepping into the story. The result is that hope, peace, joy, and love have room to grow inside us, reshaping how we think and how we respond in our daily lives.

For the next four weeks, leading into Christmas Day, let's slow down and savor the mysterious, living reality of Jesus-come-to-us, believing that as we make space for the story of Christmas, the habits we build and the holy imagination we cultivate may just transform us along the way.

How to Engage This Book

This book is divided into four weeks of reflections, poems, and spiritual practices. Each week will focus on one of the four traditional themes of Advent: hope, peace, joy, and love. As you engage with these themes, you may find that you have more connection to what you're experiencing at church when the Advent candles are lit each Sunday. My prayer for you is that this book will deepen your experience of the presence of the Spirit, who is faithful to come close to us, often through those very gifts of hope, peace, joy, and love.

Many of the devotions in this book will take the form of either long-form reflections or step-by-step spiritual practices. I wrote the book this way because I crave variety in my time of prayer and meditation. I want to offer that to you as well.

Two or three times a week, you are invited to join me in dwelling with one or two Scripture passages that will shape our reflection. At least one of the passages will be included at the beginning of each entry, though others may surface along the way. If you want to deepen your experience, I recommend you open your own Bible or Bible app and read the passages I mention with curiosity and openness.

The spiritual practices will often require creativity or embodied prayer. Many of us have been taught that the act of prayer requires sitting and thinking of the right thing to say to God. But there's freedom in releasing the expectations we often have for ourselves, particularly around whether our prayers are "good" enough. I want you to experience freedom when you come to the presence of the divine. Sitting still is good, and so are words. But God is not bound by our thinking minds. Feel free to use your body (walking, breathing, coloring, writing, etc.) and imagination when you connect with God, remembering that every part of our lives can be sacred if we invite the Holy Spirit to join us.

As you move through the practices, it will help to have a journal handy to draw in or make note of your insights or moments of connection. If you're not sure you're doing it right, welcome to the club! Connecting to God is a muscle we build by showing up and giving it a go. I hope you'll let go of the need to be perfect and experiment with ways of encountering the divine. Jesus said the Spirit of Truth will take us by the hand and guide us into all truth (John 16:13 Message). What a thing to promise. Maybe we should see what happens if we take hold of that hand.

How to Read a Poem Prayerfully

In addition to practices and prose, this book contains poems that I will ask you to engage with prayerfully.

Poetry can be intimidating, but I find it helps to think of a poem as a concentrated story, moment, or feeling told through rhythm, image, and metaphor. That concentration is exactly what can make poems so difficult to read. Imagine you're a person who has only ever seen water in liquid form. If you're handed an ice cube, you might not know what to do with it. But if you have a guide who offers you a plate to set it on, takes you outside, and shows you how an ice cube melts, you would probably think, *Oh, I get it!*

In that sense, think of the poems here as an ice cube version of ideas and language, perhaps in a form a little more condensed than you're used to. In their concise nature, these poems may reveal something fresh about the nativity story, a new perspective we might otherwise miss because we are so familiar with the narrative. In other words, give each poem a little time and patience, and it might just melt into something that moves you or awakens your imagination.

Reading a poem can take energy and awareness, and it will ask you to make connections. Here's another metaphor from my friend Molly, who teaches her college-level literature students that poetry is about evoking the senses: "It's like walking into a cozy room—you may not know exactly why it feels that way at first. But then, as you look around, you notice the dark paint on the walls, the fuzzy blanket on the couch, the soft glow of a candle, and the texture of the rug." So the smaller details create the overall feel of the room, that comfort and warmth you noticed when you first walked in. That's why poetry asks us to slow down. If we rush through the room, we probably won't have time to notice the vibes.

Poetry asks us to take our time, which requires a muscle our modern lives usually don't ask us to access. Our culture praises us for accomplishing the most in the smallest amount of time and teaches us to crave the small dopamine rewards of constant productivity. That's why the average attention span dropped from two and a half minutes in 2004 to forty-seven seconds in the early 2020s.[1] So of course reading a poem is difficult! Just as strengthening any muscle that we haven't used for a while takes effort, building up our attention may take some work.

But when we practice slowing down in order to explore the room of a poem, we are building the same muscles of attention that we need for prayer. Consider what prayer asks of us—to quiet our bodies and notice the presence of God, to pay attention to our feelings, thoughts, and embodied selves and what those things might be telling us. We offer these responses to God. And then we stay with God's presence as we look closer at those longings and consider what comes next. These are practices that melt the ice cubes into something drinkable. In that sense, poetry can be a meaningful addition to a life of prayer.

So let's get practical. Here are some tips for how to engage with these poems.

- **Keep in mind: All the poems in this book are either about Mary or in Mary's voice.** It will help you engage with the poems if you remind yourself of this as you approach them. Ask yourself about the narrator in each poem and consider how this affects your experience of the story. How is the speaker's experience revealing something new about the story of Advent you may not have noticed before?
- **Read the poem slowly**, aloud if you can, taking time to look around "the room." Do you have an emotional response? It can be positive or negative. Or neutral. Just try to notice. Then go back and read it again, giving your attention to the words, phrasing, rhythm, and structure. Take a second to wonder about how those things may have led to your first emotional response.
- **Read through it again**, maybe this time just in your mind. Is there a feeling or moment that stands out to you? Or maybe there's a word or character or image that disturbs you. Why do you think you're drawn to or repelled by these things?

- **Read through the poem once more**, asking yourself what God might be showing you through this text. Respond to what you notice in whatever form you most connect with—perhaps through journaling, drawing, or quiet prayer.

Cast of Characters

Here's who we will meet—or meet again—throughout these pages.

- A Creator who so longs to get close to creation that God takes on flesh and settles into humanity in a pretty logical way, all things considered—through a uterus. After all, how else does anybody show up in the world?
- A woman, simple and working-class, young and unwed, living under the rule of an oppressive empire, who consents to give birth to the child her people have been waiting for.
- An infant named Jesus, whose life sets off a religious revolution when he eventually claims to be the Son of Man: the most real human who ever was or will be. This humanity was not simply molded in the image of the divine but actually the embodiment of the divine, more than a reflection of Divine Love—the

incarnation of Divine Love. God here with us, present in the flesh.

- A man named Joseph, trying to be a good guy and fumbling in his attempts, yet brave enough to listen to the wise voice in his dreams, rejecting the advice of the community.
- Shepherds, slack-jawed, gazing at the sky, angel afterglow still imprinted in their eyes.
- Mystic kings trusting their knowledge of the stars and their hope for a sacred message.
- Mary's cousin Elizabeth.
- Mary's probable midwife.
- The folks who offered up their home's lower room where Mary could give birth alongside that family's animals sheltering for the night.
- Angels. Wow, so many angels.
- And you, returning to this story, willing to place yourself in it. You are invited to join the commotion and the cosmic shake-up.

WEEK ONE

Hope

Hope . . . has nothing to do with wishing. It references reality at every turn and reveres truth. . . . Hope, like every virtue, is a choice.

—Krista Tippett, *Becoming Wise*

DAY 1

Hope Begins with Looking Up

> The angel went to her and said, "Greetings, you who are highly favored! The Lord is with you." Mary was greatly troubled at his words and wondered what kind of greeting this might be. But the angel said to her, "Do not be afraid, Mary; you have found favor with God."
>
> —Luke 1:28–30

On December 12, 2022, almost one year after my dad passed away, I lay on an exam table on a frigid day in New Jersey in a hospital gown while the breast specialist cut into my body. Two days later, I flew back to my hometown to spend the anniversary of my dad's death with my mom, siblings, nieces, and nephews. I didn't tell my mom that my breast was bandaged, that tissue had been extracted, that I was waiting to learn if I, too, had cancer, one year after cancer had taken my dad.

Instead, my mom and I went Christmas shopping. We planned a family dinner—pizza and banana pudding—my dad's favorites. And I lived in the in-between for those few days, waiting. In every shop, Bing Crosby and Amy Grant crooned on repeat, and at night my hometown lit up. But in those early weeks of Advent, I felt much closer to sorrow than to hope.

I thought often of Mary's annunciation story, the words the angel speaks to her in the first chapter of Luke. She is called the "highly favored" one, but that doesn't mean she isn't unsettled by God's messenger. I know what it is to feel disquieted, to carry in my center a bodily vibration of anxiety, the kind you can't shake by shopping or chatting or ticking tasks off a to-do list. That week as I grieved my dad and waited for my diagnosis, I wasn't moved at the thought of angel choruses or shepherds keeping watch in the fields. I didn't meditate on wise men arriving with gifts. But I did find myself returning again and again to Mary: trembling at the sight of the angel, struggling through morning sickness alone, learning to embrace the news that would certainly change her life.

The Scripture readings for the first week of Advent always surprise me. Those of us who show up at any liturgical church the Sunday after Thanksgiving may find that the Scripture reading doesn't quite fit the mood of the Target where we just spent the past day snagging deals. (Or, if we're not that into Black Friday sales, the Hallmark Christmas movies we've been bingeing all weekend.) In fact, if we come to church straight out of Thanksgiving expecting an on-ramp to good cheer, we just might find that the first week of Advent is instead pointing us to some of Jesus's hardest sayings. No babies or cows in stables. Only apocalypse.

We usually think of apocalypse as destruction, but in its original sense, *apocalypse* means an unveiling or disclosure. It's the revelation of what was previously hidden, when we finally see the really real around us, the nature of things as they actually are. That year, in my grief and fear, I longed for apocalypse, for God to press through the thin places and show me what was steady in my wobbly life.

Around that time, my pastor preached on one of those disconcerting apocalyptic Jesus passages we often hear during Advent. The passage was from Luke 21, when Jesus describes coming terror and perplexity and anguish. And then he says that when these things come, "stand up and lift up your heads, because your redemption is drawing near" (Luke 21:28).

As easy as it is to glide from November straight into the delight of hot cocoa and tinsel, December will always and forever feel like the month I lost my dad. And the unsettling readings of early December will be a balm to that sharp sting in me. I know I'm not alone. So many of us need the sort of spiritual nourishment that only the waiting and wondering of Advent can provide.

Every given church on a Sunday morning holds people shaped by suffering and loss. And in this season in which we sing of peace on earth and joy to the world, that loss often rises back up to the top of our awareness. The nostalgia and beauty of the season can remind us of everyone and everything that is missing from our lives. There is power in learning to hold our own sorrow and fear alongside the sweetness of Christmas.

After all, the story of Jesus's birth begins with a whole lot of perplexity, a whole lot of anguish. The one word we're given in Luke 1 about Mary's experience upon the visit of an angel is "troubled." Her reward for being highly favored in the eyes of God is to have her life turned upside down. She runs away from her own parents, is rejected by her betrothed. She loses the trust of her fiancé and, we can assume, of her parents as well. This is not an easy story. Her *yes* to the Spirit of God costs her everything.

Mary is troubled and we are troubled. The world is shaken and Mary is shaken. We are being asked, in this and every season of Advent, to be brave. To follow the example of Mary, who, when given the choice, opens her life to the Messiah, despite being troubled, despite her fear, doubt, and sorrow.

The first week of Advent is referred to as the Week of Hope. It's the week we're invited to pause in the midst of the challenges of our lives, and the commercial hustle that invades these early days of December, and ask ourselves how we are practicing hope in our lives. The Advent readings remind us that we don't practice hope by trying harder.

In her book *Waiting for God*, Simone Weil describes our attempts at elevating our souls as akin to jumping all day long in hopes of finally reaching heaven.[1] That, of course, is not how spiritual transformation works. Instead, Weil suggests that if "we look heavenward for a long time, God comes and takes us up. He raises us easily."[2]

This is the mystery of hope. We don't discover hope in the middle of heartache by gritting our teeth and jumping higher. Weil quotes the ancient Greek thinker Aeschylus, who said,

"There is no effort in what is divine."[3] What was the effort Mary put into reaching the divine? She looked up. She saw the angel and listened. Doing so made her life a lot more complicated, but the result was remarkable.

"There is an ease in salvation more difficult for us than all efforts," Weil writes.[4] Sometimes the easy thing is the hardest thing, because it requires that we stop working so hard to grasp it and simply allow God to lift us up.

That year, as I waited for my biopsy results and grieved the loss of my dad, I was taken back to that sermon: Jesus talking about fire and terror, "the roaring and tossing of the sea," and also Simone Weil's idea that to receive the hope of God we simply stop striving, we say yes. My pastor had explained that the ease in redemption is a bit like a fiancée's "yes" to a proposal. It is "an act of attention, an act of consent. It's not a muscular effort; it's turning our head in the direction of the invitation. Advent tells us to stop, to pause, to put ourselves in a position of consent."[5]

What did Mary know of what her consent would mean for her? What did she know of loss, of fear, of the glory of her choice? This week we are invited to consider hope, and we begin by saying yes to the invitation God is putting in our path. We begin by placing ourselves in a posture of saying yes.

In Luke 21, Jesus reminds us that the worst will happen: Wars will come, viruses will mutate, loved ones will get sick, perplexity will rule. But when this happens, "stand up and lift up your heads, because your redemption is drawing near." Jesus's mother seemed to know this in her core. She didn't perform to earn her place in the story of hope. She was likely just as weak and distracted and complicated as the rest of us. But what makes her unique is how she responded in the midst of all she might lose. She said yes. And she kept on saying yes. She turned her head in the direction of the invitation.

I was in the parking lot at my favorite coffee shop when the call came in. My biopsy was clear. I laid my head on the steering wheel and cried, for myself, but also for my dad, whose biopsy had not been clear, who had lived only another eleven months after his call.

In this season, Mary is our example of how to say yes. How to choose to give our attention to the invitation. How to look up, raise our heads. Even in our grief and the ever-changing, dangerous world, there are always moments to say *yes* to the hope coming right at us, our redemption drawing near.

DAY 2

Book of Genesis

If God spoke, "Let there be light," if God simply gave
the burning spark of the sun permission to detonate.
If God said, "Let the waters under the sky be gathered
into one place," and that gathering allowed dry land.
If God is or was or can be permission to create,
then what is faith but making?

Where Mary stands—inky black, a room of eternal walls—
the light pricks through (like hope, she thinks).
"Let there be," she says to whatever is listening.
And the one who enters was always waiting
for her words. So there is.

I was inspired to write this poem after reading and reflecting on Kei Miller's poem of the same name. His poem, which I discovered through Pádraig Ó Tuama's book *Poetry Unbound* (Canongate, 2022), considers the power of creation discovered in the word "let." Kai's poem can also be found in his collection *There Is an Anger That Moves* (Carcanet, 2007).

DAY 3

What I Did / What I Hope

What is the hope you're invited to lift your head toward this week? Throughout this book I'll offer you ideas: ways to engage with the presence of God. Some will be traditional or ancient prayer practices you may recognize, and some will invite you to engage your body by walking or breathing or drawing. My hope is that these practices will offer you fresh ways to use your creativity to connect with God. Even if these practices feel uncomfortable, I encourage you to give them a try anyway. Prayer is always an invitation. We can't pray perfectly, and we don't need to. When we pray, we're simply turning our attention toward our redemption, lifting our heads in the direction of our hope.

Today we're going to try a creative prayer of *examen*. Examen is a long-standing Christian practice of prayerfully reflecting on the past day to discern the presence of God within the ordinary joys and challenges of your life. I owe the original idea for this examen to my youth ministry coleader Tim, who has been doing something similar with our congregation's high school students, drawing comics as a way to pay attention to moments of spiritual connection and disconnection.

Take a sheet of paper or open to a journal page and divide the page vertically into two columns. On one side write, *What I did*. On the other side write, *What I hope*.

Take three minutes to write all the things that happened in the past twenty-four hours: good, bad, sweet, sour. You don't have to describe every detail, just jot down the moments.

Now take three minutes to list what you hope on the other side. Maybe what you hope is the result of an experience in the other column. Maybe it's a hope for the people you've crossed paths with in the past twenty-four hours. Maybe what you hope has nothing to do with what happened or who you encountered. That's just fine. Write it down.

Take another sheet or page. Draw a line horizontally through the middle of it.

Set a timer for five minutes and use that time to draw a picture of one of the events you listed in "what I did." In this drawing, you should be the central character. You can draw it however you like, but don't worry too much about the quality of the sketch.

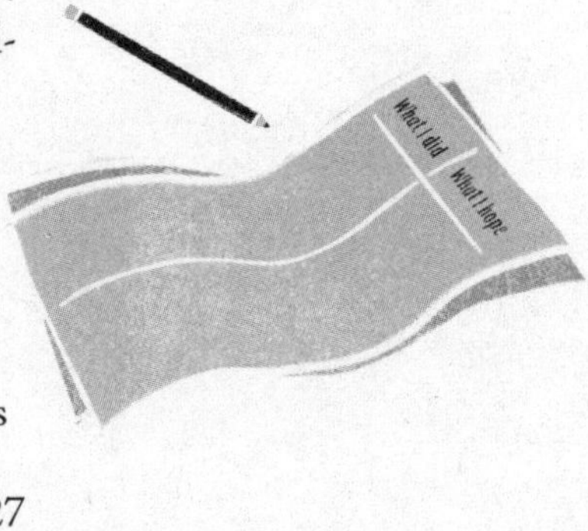

Set the timer for another five minutes. During those five minutes write underneath the sketch about what's happening in the picture. How did the people/things in this image come to be here? What are they thinking about or hoping for one another? What are you doing/feeling/thinking in the picture?

And finally, take some time to write about hope. What is your hope for the people in the sketch? What is your hope for yourself? What is God's hope for all of you?

If this has brought anything to the surface that wasn't there before, you may want to acknowledge that in prayer.

End with a couple minutes of silence.

DAY 4

Mary as Ms. Marvel

Mary has work to do. Fill the waterpots, mind the neighbor's toddler, sweep the soot. Always distracted by that plain splintered door (outside: Nazareth sheathed in dust). Mary longs to stretch time, expand her body, encircle eternity.

No, she doesn't dream of mothering. You remember fifteen, before the looking glass, longing to alter your body—pull taut the belly, smooth the thighs, reform a sloping nose? She doesn't imagine housing the divine but conceives of power beyond this material world—ground bending beneath her step, bioluminescence, unearthly speed.

Watch her ears perk when she hears the messenger near. The invitation hums—like glory—beyond earth or time. (In this scenario, the Holy Spirit will play the part of cosmic metamorphosis mist.)

Don't look too close; you won't believe it. Mary opens the door to swirling galaxies, glory's loop perpetual. Of course she drops the broom, shape-shifts to hold everything. (By which we mean God.) She extends herself to carry all the sacred mist can build. She shapes the child who remakes the world.

DAY 5

Hope Begins with *Yes*

And Mary said:

"My soul glorifies the Lord
    and my spirit rejoices in God my Savior,
for he has been mindful
    of the humble state of his servant.
From now on all generations will call me blessed,
    for the Mighty One has done great things
        for me—
    holy is his name.
His mercy extends to those who fear him,
    from generation to generation.
He has performed mighty deeds with his arm;
    he has scattered those who are proud in their
        inmost thoughts.
He has brought down rulers from their thrones
    but has lifted up the humble.
He has filled the hungry with good things
    but has sent the rich away empty.

> He has helped his servant Israel,
> remembering to be merciful
> to Abraham and his descendants forever,
> just as he promised our ancestors."
>
> —Luke 1:46–55

When we imagine Mary, we often see her as mild, saintly, and definitely unbothered by the whole angel visitation. But Scripture gives us a different image. The one word we're given in Luke 1 about her experience with a visiting angel is "troubled." We're left to use our imagination to understand what happens next. How do Mary's friends, neighbors, or family members react to her news? Do she and Joseph have a conversation, or is everything handled through her parents? Does she leave for the home of her cousin Elizabeth with the permission of her mother and father, or does she run away?

Here's what we don't have to guess at: After saying yes to all the coming trouble, Mary envisions justice breaking into our chaotic and inequitable world through the Messiah—future prophet and holy agitator—who's being formed within her. In her poem, she quotes Hebrew scripture. She insists that the story of God's work in the world is one of lifting up the oppressed, of meeting the desperate and basic needs of those who live in poverty. The song she sings in the first chapter of Luke is more than a song of worship; it's also an act of resistance.

In her book on Advent, theologian Kelley Nikondeha imagines Mary's world of poverty under the oppressive hand of the

Roman occupying force in Palestine and how Mary's courage to defy that tyrannical power is as much a part of the story of Christmas as any angelic song. Nikondeha writes, "From deep pain would now come *impossible* goodness for the world."[1] In her poem, the Magnificat, Mary insists that God's peace will find its home in all the places "where life wasn't working, where people hurt most, where hope was on the run."[2] Mary understands the longing for God's peace in those very places, because she deeply knows hurt and hopelessness.

During this first week of Advent, we are invited to take a long look at hope, which isn't naive thinking, or a promise that everything will work out in the end. Kate Bowler describes hope as being "like an anchor that's dropped way in the future. And I'm just, along with everyone else, being slowly pulled toward it." She sees hope as the belief that ultimately the story we are in is good—not just for us as individuals but for all humanity.[3]

Mary's song points to this sense of being pulled along toward something good and holy. She sings with a vision of a good story being told by divine love, a story that connects her to God's work in the past and the future. Mary's consent to carry the child from God is born of a hope that the divine is already at work upending the injustice of the world, bringing down "rulers from their thrones" and giving power to the humble. She points to the hungry being filled, while God "has sent the rich away empty" (Luke 1:53). Mary envisions God's justice as a force that moves everyone toward mutual liberation. Those who have been discarded by society are given dignity, allowing a girl like her, pregnant outside of marriage, to overcome the shame and humiliation her culture has placed on her, reversing the rules of who gets discarded and who gets to matter.[4] Hope does not require cheerfulness or assurances that all will be made easy. Instead, hope has a long lens. It has to do with connection and attention. And if we consider Mary as our example, we need only take a look at the child she raised.

We who are in the long work of caring for and raising children know that not every value we preach shows itself in our children's or loved one's lives. But as the young people we love get older, the values we've instilled often begin to reveal themselves in surprising ways. My oldest son, August, was by my side as we walked just about every street in San Francisco for the decade plus that we lived in that offbeat and soulful city. We knew our unhoused neighbors, and it was important to me that he saw our neighbors—who were often struggling with mental health issues or addiction—as valuable, as God's beloved children. We talked to them, we gave them snacks, and we acknowledged their suffering. We loved running into Thomas, who was gentle and funny, and whose stories of flying over the city with superpowers delighted us both. When he died too soon, August, then age eight, drew a picture of our friend flying over our neighborhood, all the way to the ocean. We placed his drawing at the makeshift memorial built where Thomas's tent once stood.

As I write this, my son is seventeen and works as a barista at a local coffee shop across the street from our town square and near a shelter for our homeless and struggling population. He has the evening shift and has gotten to know a group of men who gather outside the shop, coming in for conversation and hoping for a free cup. I'm not surprised that August calls each by their name and is known for slipping them free coffee. My son's manager may not love this act of hospitality, but my son's generosity makes me profoundly grateful. As a parent, I've missed the mark in many ways, but this value I hoped to pass on is rooted deeply in him. In seeing these men as people worthy of his time, my son is living out his belief that the most vulnerable among us are deserving of care and attention.

Where do we think Jesus formed the values that eventually led to his powerful Sermon on the Mount? We don't need to look further than Mary's Magnificat to see her influence on her son. Jesus's courageous and wise young mother taught him the power of a God who brings hope to the least of these. Her teaching helped lead him to the heart of the good news he came bringing. Perhaps the blessings he would one day offer in the Beatitudes were formed as his own body was forming—his vision of the poor and the meek, the grieving, and those rejected by culture as the ones blessed by God.

Mary, a teenager unmarried and pregnant, is the one who announces a cultural revolution, allowing her social vulnerability to point to the power of God's work among those deemed unimportant. As Nikondeha explains, Mary sings not only of her own blessing but also of the delivery of her people. In her song, the proud are brought low and the strong dethroned, while the humble like herself are raised up.[5] Mary seeks a new kind of justice—restoration—and Jesus would follow her path, learning from his mother that when God brings rightness and justice, the hungry are filled with good things.

Blessed are those who are hungry for rightness and justice, we hear Jesus later preach to the crowds. Rightness and justice are the backbone of the story he was born into. A mother was shamed and still given a voice among the matriarchs of her faith. A woman celebrates the lofty ones being brought down and the God of Israel ushering in a new way of liberation—one that comes through peace, the undoing of the suffering of her people under the thumb of Roman occupation. And she does it through song, with a spirit of restoration.

"Blessed is she who has believed that the Lord would fulfill his promises to her!" Mary's cousin Elizabeth declares when Mary arrives at her door—pregnant, humiliated, alone (Luke 1:45). Hope is having eyes to see the blessing before us, even if it looks like "trouble."

The way of Mary is the way of hope: believing that peace is being unfurled through God's long arm of justice, that those who are most oppressed are the ones most seen by the Holy One, and that the story of Love in the world is still offering dignity to the suffering, the misunderstood, the shamed. This is our invitation to hope as well: an invitation to seek justice—to hunger and thirst for rightness and goodness in the world. We too can choose to believe that those who, like Mary, live under violence and oppression will be restored, and we can be part of that miracle here and now.

DAY 6

Pockets

What I carried was a little paradise of my own.
In my pocket—a white shell, a wooden doll cup,
dried lavender from the garden—now spread on the table
in my silent house. This from the sea I once saw—cobalt
as wide as the sky. This tiny goblet carved for a doll's lips.
And this, dried violet buds of the field, the fragrance of my hands.

There is no telling how a people survives—
wars and rumors of wars, droughts, enslavement,
now the occupying soldiers. My people speak
of paradise as survival: Messiah advancing

This poem was inspired by a poem by Roger Robinson called "A Portable Paradise" in his book by the same name, published by Peepal Tree in 2020. To learn more about Robinson's poem, see tomorrow's practice, "See My Pockets, Lord."

with the army of David, to resume the forever story.
Trumpets of Gideon, Roman walls shook to stones,

and then peace. But I imagine lavender—fields of soft
blue,
bees humming with the breeze like a sea's tide,
in and out. Lavender oil blessing our heads,
wooden goblets filled with the juice of wild plums.
What is religion but the ruthless grip of hope?
I keep it in my pocket—lavender, the shell, the small cup.

And so when the sky blasts open
I am at the table, paradise spread before me,
windows lit with cosmic brilliance, dustlight
shimmering the surface of the wood,
I only raise my head to the angel. I do not bow.
I don't look away from the flame, the blazoner.
See my pockets, I say to the angel, *I am ready.*

DAY 7

See My Pockets, Lord

The poem we read yesterday was inspired by a poem by Roger Robinson called "A Portable Paradise." It's the final poem in Robinson's collection by the same name, a collection that addresses the tragedy of Grenfell, a tower of apartments in London that housed mostly Black and Brown and working-class tenants. In 2017, the entire building burned from what could have been a small, containable fire, killing seventy-two people. Robinson's poems address the injustices that led to the tragedy: the unequal distribution of risk and resources, an economic system that benefits some and burdens others, generational inequity, and substandard housing disproportionately affecting the poor.

Robinson's poem is written as a kind of comfort to those, like himself, who have lived lives of economic hardship. He tells his readers to carry their paradise concealed, always with them, so it can't be taken. And then, in moments of distress, he instructs readers to "empty your paradise onto a desk" and allow the light to illuminate those items as an act of confident assurance in a good future.[1]

What if Mary had been given the same wisdom? What if her grandmother had once whispered this similar advice to her? How might she carry her paradise, her hope for herself and her people, in her pockets? I wanted to imagine what she would have dreamed, what she would have kept close and spread on the table as a comfort.

As I sat down to picture Mary, I imagined her as someone who loved lavender fields. Maybe she was comforted by the smell and sight of lavender, reminded of life as it should be. Perhaps she carried a memory of the natural world, her visit to the sea as a child, and an item of joy from her girlhood, her doll's cup, knowing that she was most likely only a handful of years past carrying a doll herself.

For our practice today, I'm inviting you to return to yesterday's reading. Return to the poem, look back through the poem slowly, allow yourself to notice what images come to mind after reading the background of my own inspiration as the poet.

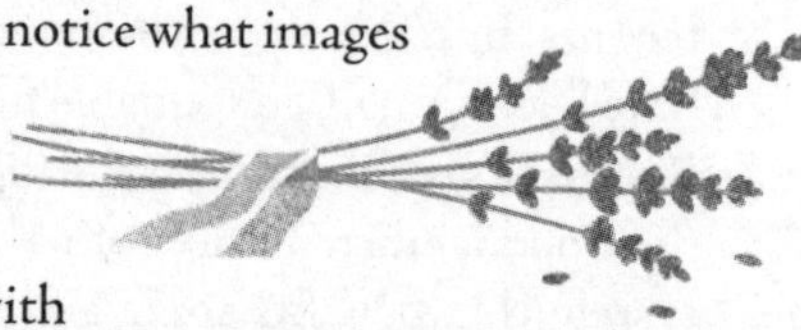

After taking time to sit with the poem again, consider these questions in the presence of God:

- What items bring me comfort, nostalgic joy, or a reminder of an important life event? Is there an item in my life I turn to for solace when I'm experiencing stress or grief?

- If I were Mary and were considering my dream of the world as it should be, what items would remind me of that greater vision?
- What feelings come up when I imagine Mary's encounter with the angel and her three items before her? Does this image bring up anything for me?

Now put this imaginative work into practice. Walk around your home or neighborhood and collect three small items that remind you of the hope you carry in your life. For today, I invite you to bring along those items wherever you go—in your pockets or purse or tote bag. When you are reminded of them, pause what you're doing and pray:

- Pray for the courage to pursue the hopes you carry and the courage to hold on to them.
- Pray for a world where your hopes can be made manifest.
- Pray that you will be a presence of hope to the people in your life.

Consider ending your prayer with these words:

See my pockets, Lord. I am ready.

WEEK TWO

Peace

The need of my heart is for room for Peace. Peace of mind that inspires singleness of purpose; Peace of heart that quiets all fears and uproots all panic; Peace of spirit that filters through all confusions and robs them of their power.

—Howard Thurman, *Meditations of the Heart*

DAY 8

The Blessing of Completeness

And he will be our peace.

—Micah 5:5

For he himself is our peace, who has made the two groups one and has destroyed the barrier, the dividing wall of hostility.

—Ephesians 2:14

For to us a child is born,
    to us a son is given,
    and the government will be on his shoulders.
And he will be called
    Wonderful Counselor, Mighty God,
    Everlasting Father, Prince of Peace.

—Isaiah 9:6

We moved to San Francisco when my oldest son was starting his second year of preschool. Our home for almost eleven years, San Francisco is a beautiful city with a wildly high cost of living. Our two-bedroom apartment was nearly 40 percent of our monthly income, so the cost of paying out of pocket for preschool was too staggering for me to get my head around. Thankfully, I had a crew of mom friends who were in the same boat. They had been in the city long enough to know about an underutilized citywide program that covered the cost of preschool for families like ours. It took only a bit of research into the program to find a small, sweet preschool for August within walking distance of our apartment. It was called Shalom School and was attended mostly by Orthodox Jewish families, with a few non-Jewish neighborhood kids like my son tacked on.

August loved his teachers, friends, and all the new holidays that entered his life at Shalom School. (Purim, with its costumes and raucous rereading of the story of Esther, was his favorite.) Each Friday, his class baked tiny challah breads to bring home for Sabbath dinner. I'd pick him up in the late afternoon to a round of "Shabbat Shalom!" from teachers to parents, from kids to teachers. It was August's favorite day of the week. We'd walk home and heat up his bread in the toaster oven, while he and his two-year-old brother, Brooks, ran around the living room yelling, "Shabbat Shalom! Shabbat Shalom!"

There was a public park beside the school where many of the kids gathered to play before we headed home after school each day. I found myself pushing swings beside Orthodox moms in hair coverings and long skirts, suddenly aware of how revealing my yoga pants were. For all that I had studied of the Hebrew scriptures as a good Christian girl, I found myself mesmerized by the rich and generous ways my new acquaintances organized their lives around their faith. I particularly loved that they had no need for shallow greetings, no "What's up?" and "How are you?" with vague and superficial responses. Shalom covered everything they needed to say in passing.

When many of us think of peace, we imagine a steady nervous system or the absence of conflict. Yet Scripture imagines something larger. The Hebrew understanding of shalom speaks of wholeness and restoration—the fulfillment of creation, the presence of justice and goodness in the world and in ourselves. Shalom is the ultimate dream of God and a blessing offered to those we pass.

As we explore peace during this second week of Advent, it's essential for us to understand peace as the people of the nativity story would have understood it. When we claim that Jesus fulfills the prophets' longing for a Prince of Shalom, we are claiming that Jesus is this presence of shalom (Isa. 9:6). He is the fulfillment of creation, the embodiment of justice and goodness both in the world and within us.

As Paul writes to the church in Ephesus: Jesus himself is our peace. Paul writes in Greek, using the word *eirēnē*, which would have been his translation of shalom from the Hebrew scriptures. When Paul writes that Jesus is the embodiment of what we translate as peace, he is tapping into that Jewish imagination of shalom. In Jesus, he is saying, we find both personal integration and collective unity. In Jesus, we find our frantic heartbeat steadied in the arms of a friend, our human propensity to misunderstand replaced with humility and mutual generosity, our impulse to hoard transformed into concern for the common good. In Jesus, we find who God has always intended us to be. "Shalom," we say to one another, by which we mean, *May you find all you were meant to be, may your body and soul be in communication with each other, may your relationships be steady and generous.* When we sing of peace on earth, we who celebrate the arrival of Jesus are claiming his very presence as the blessing we pass to one another.

Shalom has always been understood as far more than the absence of conflict or personal distress. True peace cannot be merely cultural or personal serenity. It is fierce and muscular and requires a restoration to wholeness. This sort of wholeness, Walter Brueggemann writes, "is the supreme will of the biblical God."[1]

As I write this I'm traveling home from visiting my mom during her ongoing treatment for cancer. It is one thing for my mother to be diagnosed with cancer; it is another to be diagnosed only a few years after losing my dad, her husband of almost fifty-two years, to brain cancer. The treatments she is undergoing have forced her to relive brutal memories of caring for my dad through his own illness. Reliving your beloved's suffering in your own body is too much for anyone to carry alone. As I've prayed for my mom to be at peace in both her body and her soul, I've recognized that the peace I'm asking for is more than a calm mind or a prayerful heart.

My mom needs to feel grounded in her body, drawing courage to face the mundane needs of her days. She needs the ability to calm her anxious thoughts in the middle of the night. She needs family and friends to remind her that she is loved, important, and honored. She needs her CrossFit community—athletes who are sixty years and older—to encourage her to show up and work out when she feels too exhausted to get off the couch. She needs meals made for her when it's too much to cook for herself. And of course, she needs help navigating the endless pages of insurance statements, fine print on medication labels, medication assistance applications, and pill organization.[2] Peace is more than a calm mind. Peace is an integration of community, mental and emotional support, and a physical body that can seek out comfort in the midst of distress.

As we enter this week of Advent, with its theme of peace, we are being invited to something better than the "silent night" that many of us sing about on Christmas Eve. Jesus promises to be our wholeness-maker, the one who steps into this world and actively works to bring all things together into completeness. Amid political tumult, deep social divides, and deeply ingrained biases around who is in and out, good and bad, with us or against us, our communities need a kind of peace that takes shape in the way of Jesus, a way of vulnerability and mutual humility. Our culture has taught us to hustle, to ignore our bodies for the sake of success, and to comfort ourselves with an endless feed of social media. But Advent invites us to move beyond our culture's values and into the shalom of Jesus. We begin to move toward that wholeness when we invite all the parts of us—body, mind, and soul—to be in kinship with one another, and when we labor for a world where humanity seeks the collective good in all things.

Advent is a season to use our sacred imagination, to ask the Holy Spirit what the Prince of Shalom might want to do in our lives and relationships, to open ourselves to the reality that what we do to create justice in this world reveals our beliefs about the Jesus we celebrate in this season. What blessing of shalom will you bring to the people in your life this season? What blessing of shalom will you offer to yourself?

DAY 9

The Ridiculous Everything

Suppose there was a new world, an alternative universe holding together all that flies apart—democracy, farm co-ops, marriages, bodies. Suppose the reporter yapping through the sound box in the kitchen spoke of our reclaimed bits—I mean the rising of the dead, salvaged cancered organs, wombs finally filled. Suppose death could be untaken, bleeding-out reversed, hateful words disappeared. Suppose we found the spell to hold ourselves together, a secret code that moves us toward every happy ending. Suppose we imagine this different world, learn to believe in the ridiculous everything, drag ourselves toward it, patch our sagging souls with hope.

DAY 10

Lectio Divina

Lectio divina, roughly translated as "sacred reading," is an ancient practice of prayer. This prayer practice can be traced back to the third century, particularly in the writings of Origen, who encouraged his followers, "Study these divine works with a believing and God-pleasing intention, knock at that which is closed in them and it shall be opened to you."[1] *Lectio divina* helps us to approach Scripture slowly and deliberately, repeating the passage and ruminating on it. We listen to the voice of the Spirit coming in the words, believing that God wants to speak to us through the passage on a soul level, beyond our typical intellectual response.

As we come to a passage of Scripture repeatedly and slowly, asking God's Spirit to bring something meaningful to the forefront of our thoughts or emotions, we then pay attention to the feelings or curiosities that rise to the surface, eventually asking the Spirit to help us make sense of what we might take away from our time of meditation.

Today, let's spend some time reflecting on Isaiah 52:7–10 (NASB), included below. As you begin, you may want to pray this breath prayer:

Breathe in: *Here I am.*
Breathe out: *Spirit, bring good news.*

Read this passage all the way through one time—slowly, and aloud if possible—without looking for an intellectual or emotional response.

> How delightful on the mountains
> Are the feet of one who brings good news,
> Who announces peace
> And brings good news of happiness,
> Who announces salvation,
> And says to Zion, "Your God reigns!"
> Listen! Your watchmen raise their voices,
> They shout joyfully together;
> For they will see with their own eyes
> When the Lord restores Zion.
> Be cheerful, shout joyfully together,
> You ruins of Jerusalem;
> For the Lord has comforted His people,
> He has redeemed Jerusalem.
> The Lord has bared His holy arm
> In the sight of all the nations,
> So that all the ends of the earth may see
> The salvation of our God.

After you've read through this passage once, take a deep breath, reminding yourself to move slowly in this moment of prayer. Invite the Holy Spirit to illuminate some part of the passage, allowing it to stand out more vibrantly than the others. Read a second time, aloud if possible, stopping every couple lines to slow yourself down. After you've read through it, ask yourself, *Was there an image or a word or phrase that came to mind as I read?* If so, name that image, word, or phrase to yourself, without making any judgments regarding why it came to mind.

Now, read the Isaiah passage a third time, remembering to pace yourself. This time, notice what rises to the surface for you. Is it the same image, word, or phrase from last time or something different? Reflect on that image, word, or phrase. Is there something God might be nudging you to consider based on what you've noticed in this passage? If so, name it in prayer.

Close your time of prayer by acknowledging what you've experienced. If a next step has surfaced, consider committing yourself to it. Once you've finished praying, write down that image, word, or phrase somewhere so you can keep it close this week.

DAY 11

The Slow Work of Peace

> He was in the world, and though the world was made through him, the world did not recognize him. He came to that which was his own, but his own did not receive him. Yet to all who did receive him, to those who believed in his name, he gave the right to become children of God.
>
> —John 1:10–12

> They dress the wound of my people
> as though it were not serious.
> "Peace, peace," they say,
> when there is no peace.
>
> —Jeremiah 6:14

Madeleine L'Engle begins her Advent poem "First Coming" with a line that feels more true each time I read it: "He did not wait until the world was ready."[1] Advent comes to us with so much noise it can be easy to forget that Shalom himself arrived in a world just as violent, chaotic, and anxiety-ridden as our own.

John says it this way: "He was in the world, and though the world was made through him, the world did not recognize him" (1:10). Jesus appeared on the scene when those in power were unaware of the movement of God among them. And this continues to be the case. Each Advent we celebrate the arrival of peace in human form, and each Advent it seems that few of us are ready to receive that peace.

The nativity story is one of embodied peace: God showed up in the form of Jesus, and very few noticed. But every December we tell the stories of the few who did slow down enough to encounter God's peace, those who were awake to the mystery. The shepherds got to experience the presence of love bursting out of heaven, angel choruses and all. And why? Because they were looking up at the night sky. Isn't this the case for those of us walking through Advent today? In this season it can be difficult to focus our attention on anything other than the tasks before us, the needs of the moment, the gifts to procure. How can we look to the sky for peace?

The magic of Advent is the promise that if we slow down enough to pay attention to the world beyond our material concerns, if we give ourselves the gift of unhurried attention, recognition may zing our souls. Like Mary, like Joseph, like the shepherds and wise men, when we're open and attending to the divine, we just might experience a miracle.

This is why paying attention is part of the work of the faithful. Those of us who believe that Jesus was born to be our peace are invited to live out that peace in our communities. We practice following Jesus by making space for shalom in our particular circles of influence. Peace in its full and embodied practice is never simply a passive notion, an avoidance of conflict or distress. The shalom of the Hebrew scriptures points us to the presence of something complete: the fulfillment of the Spirit of God's work among us. With that in mind, our Advent invitation is to make ourselves ready for that zing of recognition. We want to keep watch so that when the transformative presence arrives, we can be awake to the mystery of Christ's coming, a mystery that creates an active wholeness available to our relationships with others and with ourselves.

What keeps us from recognizing shalom when it lands in our lives? In Jeremiah 6, the prophet speaks of God's wrath against Jerusalem, insisting that the people of Zion must flee coming violence. This is a warning to them, that judgment is on its way to those who failed to care for the weakest among them. The voice of God points out "the wound of my people" and places judgment on the priests and prophets who didn't attend to that wound. These careless leaders and guides are saying, "Shalom, shalom," but the passage makes it clear that they're offering what my West Texan grandma would have called a whole pile of hogwash. The leaders can say "peace, peace" all they want. But if there is no peace, then they are nothing more than liars bedazzling their people's suffering in religious tinsel.

Sometimes that's what we're doing in the holiday season. We decorate the suffering or violence between us, within our communities, and within ourselves and say, "Look! We're talking about peace!" But chatter about peace doesn't equal peace.

One of my favorite poets, Gerard Manley Hopkins, put it this way, "Piecemeal peace is poor peace."[2]

I wonder if that is one reason the Christmas season can be so difficult for those who have experienced great loss or injustice. When we're suffering, dressing up our anxiety and sorrow with talk of peace is its own emotional gymnastics. We say we're doing well when we're not, simply because we're trained to hide our sorrows or refrain from placing burdens on others. We keep our conversations with those closest to us on a surface level out of fear that revealing our need will make us too much, until that boundary of shallow connection feels impossible to cross. We avoid our own inner pain because we fear the weight of giving ourselves over to it. So we distract ourselves with scrolling, with podcasts and audiobooks, with the newest Netflix show. This piecemeal peace is poor peace. Just because we decorate the world, the suffering around us hasn't been undone. Or as icon of wisdom Taylor Swift reminds us, "Band-Aids don't fix bullet holes."[3]

But what if we can hold on to a vision of peace that moves beyond the absence of conflict and instead claims the full vision of human flourishing revealed in the person of Christ? Then when we talk about peace, we can do more than dress up sorrow with religious language. We don't need to say "peace, peace," when there is no peace. Instead, the work of Advent becomes our annual chance to prepare for the entrance of shalom, to remember that we are invited to the work of peace, even if the world around us is still unready for the fullness of Jesus's coming.

We who long for real and transformative peace in a world of violence and suffering can work to build the peace we long to see. To faithfully practice Advent is to choose not to turn our gaze from the suffering we read about and witness—refugees still looking for home, immigrants pushed out of the places they once felt safe, disease and famine, child casualties of war. We who practice an unhurried connection with God can discover room in our lives to hold both the world's suffering and its hope. And we do so especially in this season of preparing for the coming of Jesus.

It can often feel like too much to attempt to carry the sorrows of our lives and communities. How can we hold pain while decorating the Christmas tree or wrapping gifts in front of a Hallmark movie? Practicing peace begins with gentleness, especially with ourselves. Unhurried practices allow us to take stock of our own needs as well as what we have to offer others. Then we can move toward opportunities to build shalom in small and faithful ways. In this way, our preparation for Christmas carries meaning beyond wrapped gifts and baked treats. We are invited to cultivate peace in our lives and in the world as we also embrace the joy of the season. To do both at the same time, we practice paying attention to the needs of our souls, the needs of those closest to us, and the needs of the world. And when we see opportunities to move shalom from our lives out into the world, we take those opportunities.

A friend texted the other day to share her experience with another family in her neighborhood. She hears their fighting and slammed doors and sees evidence of chaos. In a moment of conflict, a child from this family rang my friend's doorbell. She sat with him until his family member came outside to look for him. Her act was small, but it established for this child that her home is a safe place to seek refuge.

Another friend has cultivated a long-term relationship with the elderly neighbor next door, checking on her and inviting her into her family's life. My friend has opened her doors and her family's sometimes frenetic energy to another who would otherwise be alone.

Another friend has turned her experience raising her daughter with Down syndrome into the work of helping other families discover joy, meaning, and purpose in their experiences of disability. She does this through her own writing, podcasting, and speaking. By using her gifts, she is showing other families practical ways to celebrate the lives they've been given.

While the pain of the world may seem too terrible to move toward, we don't have to step far beyond our small circles to find others who need real and lasting shalom. We may not be able to bring war to an end or know how to tend the world's persistent poverty and violence, but we can create a space where the child down the street is welcome in a time of trouble. We can share our meals and our family with the lonely neighbor next door. We can turn our experiences into wisdom shared with others walking along a similar path.

The careless leaders of Jeremiah 6 were wasting their words of shalom by failing to practice it. But this Advent, we don't have to speak false peace where there is no peace. The songs we sing of peace this season can be for us a calling of the slow work of shalom in our small spaces of influence and care.

The shalom promised in Scripture is the active, invisible work of wholeness making its way into our bodies, souls, relationships, and communities. Shalom is something God is always creating, something we can receive and then bring to one another, something we plant and tend.

In Isaiah 52, the people of Zion are told to wake up, shake off the dust of their captivity, and remove the chains around their necks. That's when the voice of God speaks shalom, not as vain sentimentality but as a word coming from the lips of a messenger, arriving on the mountains with news that transforms everything. Those who bring peace, real peace—these are the beautiful ones (v. 7).

As we sing our songs of peace this season, may we be bearers of true shalom, not glossy religious decoration, not sentimental posing but true work on behalf of the weak and marginalized among us. May we look for where peace needs to take root in our relationships and take steps toward repair and restoration. May we look into ourselves and pay attention to the places within us that feel uneasy, incomplete, or out of sync. And may we give ourselves permission to carry peace forward with an unhurried faithfulness, like the slow work of God.

DAY 12

Bearing Peace

Even a runaway doesn't travel alone. I left on foot by caravan down the Jezreel Valley, along the Jordan to Jericho. The angel's words—*Elizabeth, your relative*—quickened in my belly. I hid the nausea as best I could. But the climb—thirty-five hundred feet in eighteen miles—sent me heaving to the bushes.

Still, I hummed a tune along the road, a poem writ in my body, my feet beat melody and rhythm into the dust. Ten days to reach my distant cousin, her face vague in memory. She waited in her courtyard, her body mid-aged and fallow, impossibly full with child. *The Lord is with thee,* she whispered. Inside her baby leaped.

What could I say? I stepped into her arms and wept. For three months we both carried wonder. Her aged skin stretched to hold her child. We gathered water, scrubbed clothes, sliced garlic and set it sizzling in the hearth. She hid me from rumors, from my angry betrothed.

The story says I sang of justice, a new Miriam proclaiming shalom for our people, calling the humble ones to rise, scatter the power mongers, empty the hoarders of their plunder. Our people have always longed for peace—creation fulfilled. That God might enclose us like a woman with child. A mother who bears good news, who hauls hope within her body.

I am afraid, I said one night beside the fire, my hand entwined with hers. My cousin's time was coming, my truth would be revealed. Will God keep the promise? Her hand brushed my cheek. *A prophetess demands shalom,* she said. *So it will be.*

Whose story is ever finished? I sang of scattered rulers, of future justice, of a people who begat mercy. One who will be our peace—like a tree by a river, a palm on a cheek, a woman who believes that what grows in us will be complete.

DAY 13

Peace Nourished by Loss

A shoot will come up from the stump of Jesse;
from his roots a Branch will bear fruit.
The Spirit of the Lord will rest on him—
the Spirit of wisdom and of understanding,
the Spirit of counsel and of might,
the Spirit of the knowledge and fear of the Lord—
and he will delight in the fear of the Lord.

He will not judge by what he sees with his eyes,
or decide by what he hears with his ears;
but with righteousness he will judge the needy,
with justice he will give decisions for the poor
of the earth.
He will strike the earth with the rod of his mouth;
with the breath of his lips he will slay the wicked.
Righteousness will be his belt
and faithfulness the sash around his waist.

The wolf will live with the lamb,
the leopard will lie down with the goat,

the calf and the lion and the yearling together;
    and a little child will lead them.
The cow will feed with the bear,
    their young will lie down together,
    and the lion will eat straw like the ox.
The infant will play near the cobra's den,
    and the young child will put its hand into the
        viper's nest.
They will neither harm nor destroy
    on all my holy mountain,
for the earth will be filled with the knowledge
        of the Lord
    as the waters cover the sea.

—Isaiah 11:1–9

A year after my dad died, my niece painted an image of a tree stump for my mom. Out of the stump grows a vibrant shoot. My mom keeps it framed in a place where she can see it every time she sits in the living room. The loss of my dad was painfully transformative for our whole family. He was our solid, gentle, relational center. Without his presence, our family unit has been forced to learn to be ourselves without him. We carried not only individual grief but collective grief as well.

This is the reality we find in the beginning of Isaiah 11. The people of God had been a strong and vibrant tree, flourishing. And now they are a stump, says the prophet Isaiah. The fruit and leaves, limbs and trunk are all destroyed. All that remains is the invisible root system, and enough of a base to sit on.

Out of that grounded bit of trunk, Isaiah foretells of new life bursting forth, a shoot that will bear branches and ripen new fruit. It will develop its own root system. What was thought to be destroyed will become the foundation for something stronger and more vibrant than what had been there before.

This passage is often read during Advent as a prophecy of the coming of Jesus and is generally assumed to have been written after the people of Israel had been destroyed by neighboring Assyria.[1] In the midst of their humiliation and sorrow, something good will emerge, the prophecy promises. This "Branch" will be discerning, mighty, incisive, and attuned to the Spirit of God. He will come to bring justice and peace to the people of Israel. And when he accomplishes these things, "the wolf will live with the lamb." In other words, once the Branch has overcome the destruction of the stump, there will be a kind of peace we have never seen with our eyes. We can only imagine it.

In her book *The Understory*, Lore Ferguson Wilbert reflects on what the death of a tree offers the forest, how dying trees continue nourishing the forest floor long after their death.[2] This ritual of the forest floor is built into our ecosystem. Isaiah seems to understand this. The shoot that grows out of the stump is particularly capable of power, wisdom, and liberation of his people because of the foundation laid before it. In other words, the stump gave life to the Branch, and the Branch multiplies that life to the people of Israel.

When we think of peace, we often picture Isaiah's vision of wolves and lambs living in harmony. But peace in our own lives is often born through some kind of ending. There is a form of peace that emerges from the ending of things, a peace that settles like a rotting tree stump on the forest floor. Peace may emerge at the end, but the process of ending is always painful. "What we find when we stop . . . moving, producing, and doing the things that previously gave us standing or community or connections—is often death," Wilbert writes.[3] For all the TikTok gurus telling us to reclaim our peace by saying no more often than we say yes, very little is discussed of the pain that can come from rejecting opportunities or relationships for the sake of healthy boundaries. Choosing peace for ourselves may mean letting go of financial comfort, social ease, or even the image of ourselves we once depended on. When busyness is a commodity that defines us, the choice to pursue shalom can look like a kind of loss. But choosing peace, even if it means releasing the things that previously defined us, will always lead to more life. The tree that falls feeds the ecosystem.

Wilbert's book invites us to a slower way of being alive: a way that replicates the work of God and the work of the natural world. She writes of old-growth forests, which still carry in their soil the carbon storage, oxygen, and nitrogen of the trees that lived centuries before them. The stumps of the trees that came before are the life force for the newly emerging trees.

Perhaps the peace of God is like those old forest floors, like the vision Isaiah understood. The shalom born of the Branch from the root of Jesse is slow, remarkable, and intricate. Which is exactly how peace settles into our lives—both communally and individually. Like those old-growth forests, it's miraculous, precisely because it takes so much time.

Advent reminds us that endings are not always endings. We are invited to imagine Jesus as that Branch, emerging from the stump of what seemed lost. May we find in Jesus a kind of peace that grows slowly and nourishes all it touches.

DAY 14

Peace as Pronouncing Blessing

Today's practice is not something to accomplish in the next five minutes but a posture you may return to throughout this week and—if it resonates with you—build into your regular spiritual rhythms. We are going to practice pronouncing blessings.

Pronouncing blessings is simply saying "I bless you" to the people, places, and things that occupy our daily lives. The truest blessings are found in the simple and particular, so you don't have to say or pray something profound or poetic in order to bless someone or something you encounter in your day. As Barbara Brown Taylor reminds us, the more you become aware, the more blessings you will find.[1]

So here's what I want us to do. Let's find our own simple blessing to carry with us into our days. A blessing we can whisper to our cat when she curls into our lap, or speak into our toddler's ear when we're helping put on shoes before school.

A blessing to think silently as we approach the postal worker behind the counter or the grocery checkout clerk, or to say out loud when someone cuts us off in traffic. Here are some ideas:

> I bless you. You are a dream of God coming true.
>
> I bless you. You have been through so much to be here right now.
>
> I bless you with the overflowing love of God.
>
> I bless you with peace that comes from the nearness of God.
>
> I bless you with purpose, because you have value and dignity.

There are so many ways to pray a blessing; there are no magic words. The invitation to bless one another is found first in noticing who is deserving of our blessings—which is to say, everything and everyone. Then we go from there.

Let's take a minute to practice. Take a breath with me.

As you breathe in, use your generous imagination to consider the face or name of someone or something you want to honor. As you breathe out, simply say "bless them" or "bless him/her/them/it."

Breathe in.

Breathe out.

Let's spend some time in silence meditating on what it might look like to become people who bless.

WEEK THREE

Joy

Be joyful
though you have considered all the facts.

—Wendell Berry, "Manifesto: The
Mad Farmer Liberation Front"

DAY 15

Building Our Capacity for Joy

> Very truly I tell you, you will weep and mourn while the world rejoices. You will grieve, but your grief will turn to joy. A woman giving birth to a child has pain because her time has come; but when her baby is born she forgets the anguish because of her joy that a child is born into the world. So with you: Now is your time of grief, but I will see you again and you will rejoice, and no one will take away your joy.
>
> —John 16:20–22

In John 16, we find Jesus with his disciples in the last hours before his arrest. He has gathered them around a table, and after washing their feet and offering them dinner, he tells them the truth: He'll be betrayed and arrested that night. This is the moment for him to give his final remarks, the teaching his companions will need to get through the dark days that follow. So it might be surprising to consider that Jesus speaks of joy in this moment. Sorrow, he says, will come upon them like labor pains. But just as labor ends in the gift of new life, their suffering won't last forever. In fact, it will transform into authentic happiness. "Now is your time of grief," he says, "but I will see you again and you will rejoice, and no one will take away your joy" (John 16:22).

This is an appropriate passage for the Advent season, especially when we consider that Jesus's mother is going through the same sorrow and wild joy as the woman Jesus describes. According to Jesus, circumstances can take away our security and ease but never our joy.

I gave birth to my youngest son knowing that he would have Down syndrome. Fear and anxiety around my pregnancy and the weeks of hand-wringing that led up to his birth made bringing him into the world sharper and more luminous than my two other births, particularly at the apex of labor. My life changed between my last push and its endorphin-rushed relief. When Ace arrived, he was suddenly no longer a diagnosis I was afraid of. He was a person, my person. I thought, *Oh, it's you. I know you.*[1]

I think of Mary experiencing that same moment: the turn from fear to connection, from suffering to transformative kinship. "Oh, it's you." This is nature's most intense whiplash: to suffer and then to immediately receive the one you suffered for, to have loved someone enough to come close to death on their behalf, and then to actually hold and know the one you have loved and given your body for. Perhaps there is no greater emotional reversal than this particular form of suffering followed by radiating joy.

Jesus wants his disciples to consider the juxtaposition of these two extreme experiences: suffering on behalf of another human's life and the delight of meeting the one you love for the first time. These two scenarios rarely go together, except in the event of giving birth. But birth has something to teach all of us about joy's expression in the midst of suffering and sorrow.

If happiness is a feeling that comes when there is no pain, joy is something that stays despite the upheaval of our lives. Joy is grounded in the core of us, where God is remaking us in the likeness of Christ, bringing us home to our truest selves. The apostle Paul often wrote about joy, expressing it as a deep, spiritually rooted contentment (Phil. 4:4–11). For Paul, our joy is grounded in the love of God, something that radiates outward from the center of us, regardless of our circumstances. When Paul prays for the church in Rome, he asks that the "God of hope fill [them] with all joy and peace" (Rom. 15:13). And he makes the case that this kind of joy and peace comes through belief, that it flourishes inside us through the power of the Holy Spirit.

When Paul speaks of joy, he seems to be making a promise that there is something deeper in and through the struggle. His joy is being created as he gives God freedom to fill his inner spirit. This is joy as a fountain, goodness that bubbles out of his pain, allowing him to keep following the way of Jesus despite the suffering he faces.

Both Paul and Jesus are saying that we can grow in our capacity for joy, that we can place ourselves in situations and relationships that increase our joy, even if our level of pleasure or ease hasn't changed. This means joy isn't abstract, and it isn't just the fancier version of happiness. Joy is actually rooted in the choices we make, even as it is born of the goodness of God. Joy asks for our collaboration.

What does this mean? We find the foundation of our joy in the daily habits that create space inside us for delight. After two seasons of depression and an ever-present struggle with anxiety, I have learned what habits build joy in me: getting outside to garden or walk, exercising, taking care of the people I love, building relationships with young people, playing with my animals, keeping music and art and nourishing words in my life, prayer, connecting with friends, delighting in good food, seeking out laughter. When I start to feel disconnected from joy, I ask myself if I have left any of these habits behind.

In his poem "Manifesto: The Mad Farmer Liberation Front," Wendell Berry instructs his readers on what it might look like to create meaning, even as the world seems doomed:

> Laughter is immeasurable. Be joyful
> though you have considered all the facts.[2]

I've been thinking about this poem lately, as political violence and rage become more and more present in our society, as peace feels harder to come by. Berry's words cause me to stop and consider: How can we laugh, even when it feels like the world is ending? How can we consider all the facts and still be joyful?

Berry's poem talks of finding life in creation and choosing to live each day in a way that isn't efficient, that can't be optimized, understanding that the most meaningful parts of our lives are found in our relationships with one another and the natural world—holding the paper-thin hand of a grandmother, singing a silly song with a child, tending the roses that were planted by the strangers who once owned your house, walking a path that transforms with the seasons. Joy is found in particular and inefficient places. And because of this, joy cannot simply *exist* in the midst of suffering; it can *flourish*.

Childbirth is often dangerous and traumatic, yet every day more than 320,000 babies are brought into the world.[3] Those are 320,000 moments of suffering turned to joy. We human beings are remarkable. We can transform our pain into something beautiful. We can consider the pain of this life and still find ways to love it. Joy is the pursuit of wonder, the power of believing that God's presence is both relational and life-giving. When we delight in God's effervescent love, it bubbles out of us and onto everything we touch.

How do we grow in our capacity for joy? My pastor once explained in a sermon that "joy can unfold as playfulness. It's engaging in something for its own sake."[4] Perhaps that's exactly where we start expanding our capacity for joy. We follow Berry's invitation and love the land we live on. We spend time in places that mean something to us. We find ways to play. We grow a garden, pet a kitten, really taste our food, show up with a gift for a neighbor, connect with friends, play beautiful music in our ears. We pray to remind ourselves that God is good.

What better time than Advent to start with play and see where that takes us? Let connection and fun lead the way. Let's take winter walks with our people, dress up for parties and dance. Let's wrap presents and watch all the cheesy movies. When we do these things with an eye for God's goodness, we just might find we are participating in good spiritual nourishment. We are building our capacity for joy.

DAY 16

Motherhood

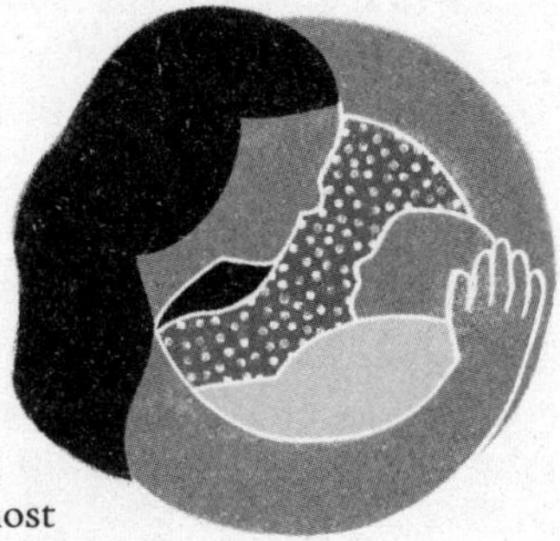

First the travail, this body host
to your animal escape.

Then the flood of release,
my center's unbearable shimmer.

I roared a broken song, a wailing psalm
until you came. And then you sang

with me. Our tears, my panting
turned laughter. Is this the way of things?

You bobbed your head at my breasts
in search of milk—ordinary, human.

My husband said, *Look at you—*
You look like a mother.

My blood trickled to the ground.
Somewhere angels shattered the sky

with glory. I wasn't seeking miracles,
no trumpets, no showers of gold.

I only ever asked for wonder. You fisted
my hair and pulled. I let you.

DAY 17

Tapping into Holy Pleasure

Pleasure tends to get a bad rap.

Our culture likes to use the word pleasure to mean superficial sexual experiences or self-centered distractions. But what if pleasure is a gift that doesn't have to remain in the realm of shallow sexuality or vain amusement? What if pleasure can be holy, can dwell in the center of God's goodness?

Take a moment to consider the things in your life that bring you pleasure. I experience it when a glass of wine slowly warms me from within and brings out the flavors of my food, or when I laugh with friends around the table, or read a great children's chapter book aloud to my little guy at bedtime. What experiences of goodness are building meaning in your life?

My fourteen-year-old son, Brooks, has played the saxophone since he was nine. He loves it so much that most of his high school experience revolves around band—marching, jazz, symphonic. I love to hear him practice and am lucky enough to have an office that shares a wall with his bedroom. He's usually careful to practice alone, recognizing that the chaos of our living room doesn't offer the quiet or lack of judgment that his room affords. But every once in a while, when he's feeling generous, he carries his tenor saxophone and sheets of music to the living room. When this happens, I'm often playing with his little brother or am around the corner cooking dinner. My home is usually filled with the deep man voices of my teen boys on FaceTime with friends, the theatrical rock of Queen (Ace's favorite), or the unnatural sounds of *Skate3* on Xbox. So for the space to be filled with jazz music, played by hands that I love? This is pleasure.

When this happens, I can't contain my delight. I wait for the song to end, then bound into the living room, whooping my pride. And if I can get past the instrument, I go in for a hug. Life with teenage sons can be tricky to manage. These days, my questions are bothersome, my requirements frustrating. I miss the moments when this boy cried for me, snuggled into my lap after school and asked me to read the same picture book every day for two years. Now, I share him with his friends, his passions, and his commitments. Sometimes he walks in the house and moves past me, eyes on his phone, forgetting to look up and say hello. Parenting is always an act of letting go. No matter how much I delight in seeing my kids thrive, watching them move on without me tugs at something tender in my spirit. That's why those moments of connecting to my son's music are more than sweet; they are among my holiest pleasures. It is sacred joy to celebrate the gifts he brings to the world, even as I carry nostalgia for the simple, chaotic days of his childhood. Despite the changes in his maturity and our relationship, when I take pleasure in his music I am carrying muscular hope for the future person he'll be. As he plays and I listen, the pleasure we both feel unites us and asks something of us. It's in that sacred connection that we grow in joy.

Joy is built on these sorts of holy pleasures that shape us further into the people God desires for us to be. What pleasures may be pointing toward God's dream for you?

Today, spend some time imagining what brings you the most joy in your daily life. Maybe it's making your bed or dancing with your person, listening to a great album, driving your kids and their friends around, or a long bath. Maybe it's eating french fries!

Answer these questions. Write down your responses, if you want, or just think them through in a prayerful moment.

- What pleasures in your life do you experience as holy?
- What pleasures do you experience as shallow, distracting, or destructive?
- Where is God present in the experiences and moments that bring joy?
- What do those pleasurable or joyful moments tell you about who you are?
- What do those pleasurable or joyful moments tell you about who or what you love?
- What do those pleasurable or joyful moments reveal about God's work in your life?

Spend time in prayer considering your answers, asking the Spirit to give you clarity around what delights you and what God may be revealing to you through those delights.

Close with this prayer: *Spirit, empower me to notice the holy pleasures in my life. Bring me into a life of joy for the sake of your dreams for the world and your dreams for me. Amen.*

DAY 18

The Opposite of Anxiety

"Surely God is my salvation;
    I will trust and not be afraid.
The Lord, the Lord himself, is my strength and
        my defense;
    he has become my salvation.
With joy you will draw water
    from the wells of salvation."

In that day you will say:

"Give praise to the Lord, proclaim his name;
    make known among the nations what he has done,
    and proclaim that his name is exalted.
Sing to the Lord, for he has done glorious things;
    let this be known to all the world.
Shout aloud and sing for joy, people of Zion,
    for great is the Holy One of Israel among you."

—Isaiah 12:2–6

One of my earliest core memories is of a frantic attempt to leave for school on time. I can still feel my scattered heartbeats, hot tears, and shaking hands as my little body sat on the brown shag carpet and I tried to shove my feet into my Keds. The tongue of one of the shoes caught on my sock. I cried "I'm late! I'm late!" while my body heaved, too worked up to actually tie my laces, my older brothers standing nearby, unmoved because they'd seen it all before.

I feel nothing but tenderness toward my disquieted seven-year-old self, clearly troubled, but the 1980s was a cultural moment when kids like me simply weren't treated for anxiety. Despite this, my adult-diagnosed generalized anxiety disorder is all over my memories of childhood. All of us hold painful core experiences that reveal the challenges we end up facing all our lives. In my least regulated moments as a mom in my early thirties, I was often that same little girl, just trying to get my kids' shoes on, watching the clock, berating myself for not having better control—of them, of me. Usually, the thing in us that needs the most mending reveals itself over and over until we are forced to confront it. It wasn't until I took my own child to therapy for his anxiety that I was compelled to admit he was simply mirroring me.

Therapy is where I learned the power of being a nonanxious presence, not only to my child who shares my anxiety diagnosis but also among the people I lead. Family systems theory, from which the concept of a nonanxious presence was first developed, studies how anxiety travels through a group and how one emotionally balanced leader in the system can stabilize the entire community.[1] When my church offered me a job as a youth director, "nonanxious presence" was used to describe the work I would do. Ministry to teens is far more about who we are in relationship to them than what we teach or organize on their behalf. My prayer is that I am an adult who continually shows up for the young people I lead, who actively models an unshaken belief in God's work of goodness in the world and in their lives, and who leans into joy despite the challenges of my life and invites them to do the same. This calling to be a presence of curiosity, genuine care, and yes, of nonanxiousness, is more important than any scriptural teaching that comes out of my mouth at youth group. To be a nonanxious presence is not to be perfect; it's to be joyfully human in a world that demands we live up to superhuman expectations.

We are living in a time of political binaries, when chaos rules our social media feeds, when the fear of gun violence lingers in the back of our minds as we drop the kids off at school, and when never-ending, color-coded work calendars remind us our time doesn't really belong to us after all. It's no wonder, then, that anxiety has become our culture's most consistent daily companion. How can any of us who swim in the waters of overwhelm and exhaustion become the kinds of people who move and think and respond from a place of stability, the people who walk through the world with generosity and wholeheartedness? To be a nonanxious presence is to imagine a different way of being a person.

I listened to a podcast interview with Father Greg Boyle on one of my many Wednesday night drives from New Jersey to New York City for youth group. Even over audio, the Jesuit priest and founder of Homeboy Industries so beautifully modeled the nonanxious presence I long to embody that I had to write down his words once the car finally came to a stop. His interview with Kate Bowler has stayed with me.[2]

Father Boyle has worked with recovering gang members and drug addicts for forty years, a ministry that has surely brought him great sorrow and distress. Yet as he spoke with Kate, he manifested joy. I drove that afternoon toward the Holland Tunnel, wondering how a person like Father Boyle gets formed into such a steady, generous presence. How in the world can we grow less anxious while surrounded by challenges? Is it really possible to move toward more joy and more hope in the midst of heartbreak?

When my older boys were young, I had a few prayers I said over them every night. One was this: *I pray he will love the things God loves*. This has always seemed like the clearest prayer I can pray for my children—or myself. To love what God loves: to delight in people, in creation, in goodness, in fun. To find life and satisfaction in connection, as opposed to relevance, performance, or shallow distraction.

Father Boyle's nonanxious presence in the interview revived that old prayer in my mind. Perhaps when we love what God loves, when we love the people God loves—particularly those often rejected by society—we find our way toward joy. Quoting a friend, Father Boyle said, "Once you know the God of love, you fire all the other gods." He went on to explain himself: "The other gods are the ones that are operative, saying 'it's all about you and make sure that you're happy.' . . . But the goal in allowing the folks at the margins to make you different—the goal is joy, everybody inhabiting it in an exquisitely mutual way."[3]

This statement alone could transform us all: Fire the gods who tell us that life is about stuffing ourselves with superficial pleasures, convincing our minds that shallow happiness will carry us into meaning. Fire the gods who insist upon our hurried pace and frantic nervous systems. Instead, we can choose Love itself, the God who is love, who guides us toward love, who invites us to love. Joy is found in that invitation of love, when we refuse to bow to the frenetic expectations of our inboxes, or to soothe ourselves with a relentless stream of thirty-second videos. When we seek to know the God of love, we learn to put ourselves in a position of humility and generosity, to take time to see the people we interact with, to pursue connection and authentic delight. Divine joy, Boyle says, is "exquisitely mutual."

When our daily life choices are motivated by love instead of ego, we're able to choose hope and vision for the people around us. A person who practices care for others, motivated by authentic joy, will become a transforming and nonanxious presence no matter how much pain remains around them.

Isaiah 12:2–6, a common reading for this third week of Advent, is from a passage that begins in chapter 11. In the first ten chapters, Isaiah foretells a time of great loss for the people of God. Jerusalem will be destroyed, the prophet says, and the people will be scattered to other countries in exile. In telling of this devastation to come, the writer then anticipates a day of restoration. Chapter 11 speaks of one who will come and restore all things. Then chapter 12 arrives with good news. "In that day you will say . . . surely God is my salvation; I will trust and not be afraid" (vv. 1–2).

Salvation is a word burdened with all sorts of baggage for many of us who grew up in the evangelical tradition. It can bring up white-hot memories of altar calls and nighttime anxiety-fueled prayers when we hoped God would finally accept our attempts at asking Jesus into our hearts. For us, salvation required a three-step process of believing enough, repeating the right words often enough, and having enough faith to be spiritually acceptable.

So those of us who come to these words from Isaiah on the other side of spiritual trauma may struggle to encounter the word *salvation* in the wild, outside phrases like "plans of salvation" and Romans Road tracts. It's important to recognize how the Hebrew people would have understood salvation in a passage like Isaiah 12. Here, the word simply means what it means in any English dictionary: to be delivered or rescued from danger, ruin, or loss. When our speaker in this passage speaks of salvation, they aren't expressing a spiritual experience of transcendence or eternal deliverance; they are talking of something much more immediate: rescue from their captors, their oppressors. The speaker here is practicing hope. *Surely(!) God is my salvation.* Surely I won't be stuck in this space of loss, ruin, and danger forever. Surely I will walk out of the foreign land where I've been held captive and step back into my homeland. And when the speaker clings to this hope, the result is that they learn to trust, they become unhurried and unafraid. This is antianxiety.

Walter Brueggemann writes that Isaiah 12 is "an act of buoyant and determined hope that refuses to give in to debilitating present circumstance."[4] The passage begins with this act of hope, then continues with joy: "With joy you will draw water from the wells of salvation" (Isa. 12:3). Somehow in the midst of the suffering and sorrow of being taken from their home and made refugees in other lands, the Hebrew people are promised in Isaiah 12 that they will not be forgotten. Not only will they be rescued, but their salvation will result in joy. There's no happiness mentioned here, no comfort promised. Some pain lives deep in us forever. But joy is strong enough to stand alongside pain. Joy is not afraid of all we need to be delivered from.

Again, here's Father Boyle: "You move from others-centered . . . to loving-centered. And you go, 'Oh . . . loving is my home and now I'm never going to be homesick.' And that becomes the place of joy."[5] How can we reach beyond the pain of our lives this Advent? How can we tap into the nonanxious presence we see in Mary when she sings her Magnificat, believing with all her heart that the God of her salvation will rescue her people just as was foretold in Isaiah 12—believing that she, too, can trust and not be afraid?

Her song reminds me of that prayer I spoke over my kids' sleepy bodies. In it she lists the things God loves, even as she is learning to love them too. Perhaps her soul prayed and still prays alongside Father Boyle, "May we be loving-centered; may loving be our home."

I imagine her delighted by her own joy, drawing water from the well of the salvation promised to her people. Nonanxious Mary. Nonanxious us.

DAY 19

Releasing Ego, Embracing Joy

Paul writes in his letter to the Philippians that we should "rejoice in the Lord always," inviting his readers to a wild idea that living in a constant prayerful attitude may transform our anxiety (4:4–7). When I read this passage, I imagine Paul putting his own spin on the Sermon on the Mount, in which Jesus instructs his listeners to simply be present and trusting, not worrying about what's around the corner. Instead, they can live like the wildflowers, covered in beautiful "clothes" they didn't strive for (Luke 12:22–27). When Jesus gives that same sermon in Matthew, he adds something active to the work of being a nonanxious presence (Matt. 6:33). Anxiety makes us seekers, frantic movers who need to control our lives. Instead, Jesus invites us to a counterintuitive urgency: We are to live without urgency in the ordinary details of life so that we *can* be urgent about what Jesus calls God's kingdom—the dream God has for the world.[1] In order to transform our desire for control into a longing to bring God's dream into reality, we are invited to slow down so we can live in the presence of God, delight in the things God loves, and see the people we encounter as worthy of our time and energy.

When we are urgent about God's dream for the world, we live unhurried; we release control. When we put the dream of God above all that we hope to control, our troubles of life don't necessarily fall away, but our meaning and purpose give us clarity to hold those troubles with compassion and gentle trust (Matt. 6:33). In these words of Paul and Jesus, we hear remnants of Isaiah 12:2: "I will trust and not be afraid."

All this trusting, slowing down, and dream-of-God pursuing becomes a path toward the joy described in Scripture. Perhaps joy has always been the opposite of anxiety. We begin to move toward habits of joy when we learn to practice the hard work of letting go, releasing our ego-driven responses, which, according to Father Richard Rohr, are "always an inadequate or even wrong response to the moment." How do we know what is ego and what is soul? Rohr says that the ego self-attaches itself to "mere externals" because the ego has no inner essence.[2] When Rohr explains attachment in terms of ego, he doesn't mean the things we attach to in and of themselves—relationships, identities, or possessions. What becomes a problem in our lives is the part of us that clings to these things for security, easy outcomes, or attention. When we *must* have a person or thing or status in order to be okay, a part of us is still clinging to externals rather than being formed by the softness of a healthy soul. It's important to note that nonattachment isn't not loving—it's loving without clutching. It's love without being in control.

"The soul does not attach, nor does it hate; it desires and loves and lets go," says Rohr.[3] This definition is deeply challenging for me, and for most of us! I can list so many parts of my life that I cling to, whether it's how I'm perceived or relationships I can't imagine living without. But the work of surrender asks us to release our grasp on control and move toward the surrender of real joy.

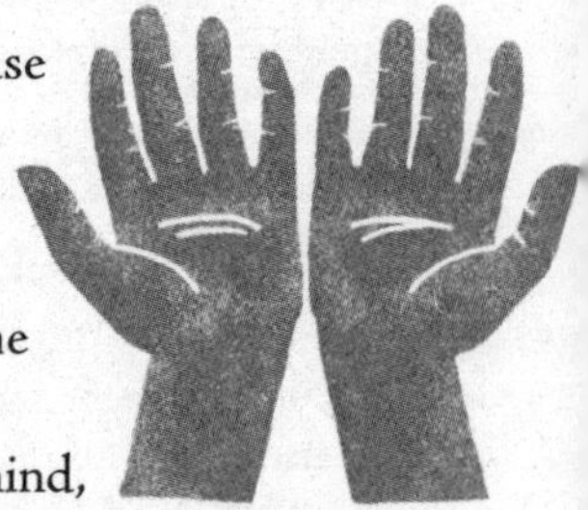

So, here's a practice that can help us release ego and embrace joy.

Spend five minutes in centering prayer. Centering prayer simply means sitting in silence and letting your body be still in the presence of God.

It helps to have a word to hold in your mind, one that you can return to whenever your thoughts stray. For this practice, I recommend you use the word *joy* as something simple to help keep you centered.

After spending those five minutes in silence, returning your mind to the word *joy* over and over, consider closing your time with a breath prayer—a simple way to be embodied in this time of prayer.

Here's an example:

Breathe in: *I turn my heart toward joy.*
Breathe out: *I let go of control.*

Breathe in: *I turn my heart toward joy.*
Breathe out: *I let go of vain performance.*

Breathe in: *I turn my heart toward joy.*
Breathe out: *I let go of petty unforgiveness.*

Breathe in: *I turn my heart toward joy.*
Breathe out: *I let go of frantic schedules.*

Breathe in: *I turn my heart toward joy.*
Breathe out: *I let go of distraction.*

Breathe in: *I turn my heart toward joy.*
Breathe out: *I let go of shallow comfort.*

Feel free to continue this prayer as long as you need in order to experience relief and remind yourself that joy is always found in the presence of God.

DAY 20

How to Bear Sorrow

The king was distressed, but because of his oaths and his dinner guests, he ordered that her request be granted and had John beheaded in the prison. His head was brought in on a platter and given to the girl, who carried it to her mother. John's disciples came and took his body and buried it. Then they went and told Jesus.

When Jesus heard what had happened, he withdrew by boat privately to a solitary place. Hearing of this, the crowds followed him on foot from the towns. When Jesus landed and saw a large crowd, he had compassion on them and healed their sick.

As evening approached, the disciples came to him and said, "This is a remote place, and it's already getting late. Send the crowds away, so they can go to the villages and buy themselves some food."

Jesus replied, "They do not need to go away. You give them something to eat."

> "We have here only five loaves of bread and two fish," they answered.
>
> "Bring them here to me," he said. And he directed the people to sit down on the grass. Taking the five loaves and the two fish and looking up to heaven, he gave thanks and broke the loaves. Then he gave them to the disciples, and the disciples gave them to the people. They all ate and were satisfied, and the disciples picked up twelve basketfuls of broken pieces that were left over. The number of those who ate was about five thousand men, besides women and children.
>
> —Matthew 14:9–21

This third week of Advent, the week when we turn toward joy, will always be the week my dad died.

I landed in my hometown the night of December 13, 2021, then spent the next day arranging in-home hospice care with my brother, signing documents, and scouring all the pharmacies of my town for pink sponge swabs. After I found them, I sat at Pops's side, soaking a pink sponge in water and offering it to my dad's closed, dry lips. I had helped him move his body to the easy chair that morning, and by the afternoon I regretted it. His bones and muscles and skin seemed lit with pain. Though his easy chair leaned all the way back, he curled sideways.

By then he had stopped talking and eating, and as the mother of a nonspeaking autistic child, I felt connected to his nonspeaking presence, as if I had been training for this moment all my mothering life. I hovered close, longing to decipher his needs the ways I deciphered the needs of my then-six-year-old son. My mom and I helped Pops walk the twenty feet toward his bed. The next morning he didn't wake for us, his body unnaturally still, limbs shutting down. He kept breathing, and the hospice nurse delivered the morphine. My brothers and sisters-in-law, nieces, and nephews all came to sit on the bed beside Pops and tell stories. We laughed and took turns covering our faces, the grief red-hot and quick. His pastor stood beside his bed and sang an old hymn. My kids and husband FaceTimed to say goodbye. That night my brothers, mom, and I each took two-hour shifts sitting beside my dad in bed. I read him the final chapter of C. S. Lewis's *The Last Battle*. He died the next morning, on December 16. We buried him December 21, sang "Silent Night" three days later. We opened presents.

In my story, Advent will forever be woven into the loss of my dad. Many of you who grieve in this season hold your own unique story of loss. Winter solstice in the northern hemisphere is an integral part of these days. The longest night of the year is simultaneously the shortest day. We twist twinkle lights through our homes and along our porch railings and thresholds because our ancestors showed us how to hold light and dark at once. We do what we learned to do from our grandparents and the ones who raised them: We light candles, we toss tinsel, we sing. These are the darkest days, and joy is how we move through them.

Etty Hillesum was a young woman in the Netherlands who worked to support her Jewish community until she was arrested, deported, and ultimately murdered in 1943. She wrote about spiritual resilience and courage in the midst of terror, oppression, and dehumanization. She seemed, impossibly, to grasp the power of tenderly carrying her own grief. From the darkness of Auschwitz, Hillesum wrote in her journal, "You must be able to bear your sorrow; even if it seems to crush you, you will be able to stand up again, for human beings are so strong, and your sorrow must become an integral part of yourself; you mustn't run away from it." She wrote to herself: "Give your sorrow all the space and shelter in yourself that is its due, for if everyone bears grief honestly and courageously, the sorrow that now fills the world will abate."[1]

I think of her words when I see Jesus practicing a similar tenderness in Matthew 14. In this passage, when Jesus learns of the brutal murder of his mentor, friend, and cousin John the Baptist, Scripture says he "withdrew by boat privately to a solitary place" (v. 13). Jesus takes time to work through his grief, removing himself from his followers and friends in order to process, pray, and cry. This is not simply a moment of loss for Jesus; it's also likely the moment he recognizes that the people in power who had no problem throwing John the Baptist's head onto a platter are coming for him as well.

Jesus gets away from his friends and followers not to teach a lesson about prayer but because he is heartbroken. He withdraws from others' expectations because he is kind to himself. He chooses to give his sorrow "all the space and shelter in himself that it is due." The Gospels are rarely good at giving us time markers, so we don't know how long he gets away. Is it only for a couple hours or for a couple days? All we know is that when the crowds of people find him and demand his attention, he's able to return to care for them from a wholehearted posture. How does Jesus encounter the beauty of richness and of the world? First, he grieves and connects to his source of love, his Father. Then he turns to the crowds with compassion. This is how he responds with a steady spirit when faced with the hunger of the people before him. This is how he taps into a miracle.

I love what comes next: not the flashy miracle that following his ego might have granted—bread falling from the sky manna style, fish flying out of the sea and landing at the feet of the hungry. Instead, Jesus is sturdy in heart in the way only a human who has suffered can be sturdy. He gives the disciples instructions and allows them to be the witnesses of the work of God, watching the bread and fish grow as the disciples give of themselves. He considers the needs of the disciples he's guiding and offers a slower way, a transformative and sacred gift. It's a beautiful picture of how miracles can flow out of pain and suffering.

This week we practice what may feel impossible for some—joy. And the joy we're asked to practice is richer, more profound than any idea we sing about at Christmastime, beyond our shallow attempts of leaving behind the pain of our lives in order to force smiles on our faces. Joy is the spirituality of stringing metaphorical twinkle lights along the railing of our darkest days. Joy is giving our sorrow room to breathe, believing along with Etty Hillesum that our pain can become such an integral part of us that it forms the foundation of our wholeness.

When I read this passage in Matthew, I wonder if this miraculous feeding would have taken place were it not for Jesus's grief. He steps away and, in doing so, finds the strength to meet the needs of his followers from an unhurried, ego-free posture. In the passage that follows, Jesus once again sends his disciples off without him, withdrawing to pray. Following that, he arrives at the sea in the middle of the night and walks across it, steadily pursuing Peter (Matt. 14:22–33).

What if the truest miracles arrive because of our pain and not in spite of it? Perhaps the greatest of all miracles is not food from above or physics-defying water-walking but joy.

At the bottom of our pain is the foundation of our joy. This is a mystery I can't explain. This is a mystery Etty Hillesum told us to look for: "If you have given sorrow the space it demands, then you may truly say: life is beautiful and so rich. So beautiful and so rich that it makes you want to believe in God."[2]

DAY 21

Joy

(for Christina)

Mother's feet shuffle through the sleeping room.
Mary staggers to support her, gripping her waist.

Take your time, Mary says. I'm fine, Mother says.
They wobble out the dark room past the courtyard

and behind the house, the family's trench,
its seat of smooth stones. Robes up, she hovers

mother above the pit. This need quotidian, relentless
as age and illness. Who can always wipe another

with joy? Mary squats beside her. I've got it,
Mother says, tries to stand, then plunges dizzy

toward her daughter, dead weight that hurls Mary
to her back. They hit the hard earth and grunt,

foreheads pressed together. I'm fine, Mother says,
then giggles. Mary holds her mother, bare-assed

on rough earth, scratched by limestone.
See! Mother snorts. Just fine!

Their laughter rises to the angels.

WEEK FOUR

Love

I'm still learning to love
and fully be human
to bring all I am
be born again
and give all my heart.
Blessed be the humanity of God.

—David Gungor,
"Blossom into Future"

DAY 22

Love Is the Container; Love Is the Story

"Teacher, which is the greatest commandment in the Law?"

Jesus replied: "'Love the Lord your God with all your heart and with all your soul and with all your mind.' This is the first and greatest commandment. And the second is like it: 'Love your neighbor as yourself.' All the Law and the Prophets hang on these two commandments."

—Matthew 22:36–40

This is how we know what love is: Jesus Christ laid down his life for us. And we ought to lay down our lives for our brothers and sisters. If anyone has material possessions and sees a brother or sister in need but has no pity on them, how can the love of God be in that person? Dear children, let us not love with words or speech but with actions and in truth.

—1 John 3:16–18

I was seventeen, on my first adventure outside the US, floating on a white and blue boat, its deck covered in bright woven hammocks where the staff slept in order to catch a breeze at night. July on the equator was thick with humidity. I finally understood what people meant when they described heat as suffocating. The Rio Negro, which joins the Amazon River in Manaus, was the largest and darkest river I had ever seen. We traveled for hours, spying river dolphins and piranhas, docking along the banks of a handful of villages whose names escape me all these years later, each town a community fully dependent on the boats like ours that made their way through the wide river, delivering goods, bringing information from the world outside.

Only a few weeks beyond high school graduation, all I longed for—besides true love—was adventure and my whole life's purpose. No pressure! I was told I had the answer for the people we would find in every village. Hard-working fisherfolk, simple farmers, families in one-room homes, their bright-colored hammocks strung up each night for sleep, then rolled tidily into the corner each morning. These folks welcomed our boat onto their shorelines, invited us to their town's afternoon soccer games, and sometimes even shared their rice and beans. We were a group of gangly teens from Texas, and we were there to tell them how to know the one true God. *Confess your sins. Believe in your heart. Pray this prayer.* We held the secret code for life's happiness in our middle-class, American, white-kid hands.

I had come to change the world. And I had hope that this one message—repent, believe—was the one that might give purpose to the world's suffering and bring peace to the most violent places. I had come with words and a three-point spiritual plan. In those ten days in northern Brazil, I didn't yet have the life experience or wisdom to understand that the people who welcomed me into their sacred spaces were experiencing lives more difficult and more deeply communal than I could see from within my own cultural lens. I was supposed to tell them how to know the love of God, yet thirty years later, I'm still learning how to tap into that love.

In our reading today, when asked about the greatest commandment, Jesus tells his listeners that the entire law and the prophets can be summarized in two statements: "Love the Lord your God with all your heart, and with all your soul and with all your mind. . . . And love your neighbor as yourself" (Matt. 22:36–40). Love of God and others becomes the lens through which Jesus wants his followers to bring their faith into focus. This love is self-giving. It is both the culmination and the container of hope, peace, and joy.

The love of God, neighbor, and self that Jesus preaches isn't sentimental or abstract. The love Jesus demonstrates in his stories and in his direct teaching is something richer and more costly than a feeling of connection. On his final evening with his disciples before his crucifixion, Jesus offers a new way of naming this kind of love—friendship. Because they are his friends, they are to love one another, he says (John 15:9–14). Jesus instructs this not because he's an overlord who dishes out rules but because the love he's inviting them to is an active thing, something that friends do. Stanley Hauerwas reminds us that "to be a friend of Jesus didn't turn out very well for most of the disciples."[1] In other words, this kind of love required that they give themselves away. And that costly love, that giving away of themselves, is another word for faith.

As we enter this final week of Advent, moving toward the culmination of the Christmas story, we come to this small, abstract, and unwieldy word—love. The writer of 1 John tells us that love is the essence of God (4:8). Jesus tells us it is the greatest of all commands. And Jesus's friends lose their very lives for the sake of it. Scripture reminds us that if we want to know what love is, we begin by considering that Jesus Christ laid down his own life (1 John 3:16).

How can we even get our heads around what it means to love God, love ourselves, and love others? Hauerwas describes the self-giving flow of love as "the very substance of the relation between the Father, Son, and the Holy Spirit."[2] Love—whatever it is—is the center of the Christmas story, the essence of God embodied.

That summer on the Rio Negro, I felt torn between the urgency of doing what I believed was God's work and the restless fear that I might never know my true place in it. All I wanted was to do it right, and by *it* I meant *everything*. I needed to choose correctly—college, career, husband—in order to please a God who knew the plan but was hiding it. I wasn't sure how to find the entry point for God's plan, but I figured a college major was a good enough place to start.

A tightly wound good girl who (still) likes to pray dramatically, I stood alone on the back of the boat on our last night on the river, imploring God to make everything clear. *Please,* I begged, *tell me how to do it right. Tell me the college major you have picked for me!* The answer that came has been my life's north star, the clearest experience I've had of a wisdom not my own—beyond the spiritual voices in my life, beyond my lived understanding, beyond my inner voice. In that moment of prayer, I heard that life was different than I had imagined it, that what mattered more than the choice of college, spouse, or career was how I embodied God's love in the world. *Look at the river,* I sensed God whisper. *Wider, deeper, longer, fuller than you could've imagined. My love is like this river. Stay in my love.*

God as water is a theme that flows throughout Scripture. Through the voice of the prophets, God is identified as "the spring of living waters" and "the spring rains that water the earth" (Jer. 2:13; Hosea 6:3). In Ezekiel, the prophet sees a river that flows from the temple and awakens the land back to life wherever it flows (47:1–12). Jesus speaks of himself as the culmination of Jeremiah's living water "welling up to eternal life" when he reveals his identity as Messiah to the woman at the well (John 4:14). Then he takes it even further in the temple during a festival, where he shouts to what seems like a room full of skeptics that if they actually chose to believe, "rivers of living water will flow from within them" (7:38).

There's an abundance of metaphors and images for God in Scripture, and if God is the actual manifestation of love, as the author of 1 John says, then these metaphors for God find themselves to be true in what Paul calls "the greatest of" the virtues, the container of the gifts that are promised to flow out of our lives (1 Cor. 13:13). When I heard that whisper on the boat, this inner knowing that God was the love that would sustain my life, I realized God was inviting me to sink my whole self into that love and let it move me. I could stop trying to solve my life like a secret puzzle I didn't have the holy savvy to grasp. Instead, I could lean back and let the love of God carry me. By resting in that love, I would be changed in the best way, eroded like a stone in a river. I would become everything God dreamed for me to be simply by letting myself be moved by God's love through the world.

Many great theologians have taken on the question of how to define love. Hauerwas says we know what love means: "Love means cross."[3] The cross invites us to joyfully give of our own comfort, pleasure, or agenda for the love of another. We do this not for what we can receive or manipulate from our actions but because we honor the other's inherent worth.

It can be tricky to name what love looks like in relationships. When the writer of 1 John describes love, he challenges his readers to recognize the fallibility of words, how the language of love can be shallow or easily manipulated if it's not backed up by action (3:18). Even if we don't see ourselves as manipulative, many of us know an early flirtatious excitement that made us feel good about ourselves until we realized we liked the feeling of being wanted more than we liked the other person. Or we can recall past experiences of friendship in which another's social capital improved our own. Even as a parent, I can puff myself up when my children make me look good. But when we use or manipulate another for what we can gain, it isn't love.

It is only when we offer authentic attention to the friend, romantic partner, or family member before us, allowing ourselves to engage with them for who they are and not what they offer, that our actions can carry the truth of love. These embodied acts of care, attention, and service can truly enrich the life of another. As we read in 1 John, we know what love is because we see the example of love on the cross. In the way of Jesus, love always costs us something.

Iris Murdoch, the great twentieth-century novelist and philosopher, described love as "the extremely difficult realization that something other than oneself is real."[4] Her definition of love is often called a "nonviolent" form of attention we can pay a fellow human. That word *nonviolent* doesn't simply mean a lack of physical brutality; it means a lack of manipulative force, in which we choose not to use another person for our own gain. To offer nonviolent attention toward another, we must fully recognize that the other person experiences life independently from ourselves. Every person we encounter is a being who exists beyond our personal thoughts, feelings, or actions. This may seem basic, but active nonviolent attention asks us to continually remember that we are not the center of the story. When we see another as an independent soul worthy of our energy and care, we refuse to use them as a mirror for our experience of life. We are able to love without using the person to meet our own desires or needs.[5]

This is the model of Jesus, that he chose to love, even with diminishing returns, all the way to the cross. When we follow this way of Jesus, not denying our own value even as we serve and care for others regardless of reciprocity, we are transformed. I recognized a glimpse of this as I gazed at the Rio Negro from the back of that blue and white boat. Life was more than solving a spiritual puzzle and something better than seeking my own best interests. It was an invitation to form my life around a transformative love that moves us all toward goodness. I was invited to know a God who embodies love, and that love would change me.

This final week of Advent, we are stepping into the greatest story of love ever told. It's not simply an equation to solve a spiritual problem, not just another tale of a holy woman giving birth or an inspirational angel legend. It's the story of love as a better narrative, a God who so embodies self-giving love that God refused to cling to divine power, assuming the utter weakness of a human infant. Christmas is the story of cosmic humility, God embodied in our form and flesh, God contained in humanity (Phil. 2:6–8). What a thing to celebrate.

This week, may we listen for the voice of wisdom that speaks beyond our understanding, experiences, or anxieties. May we find ourselves in awe of a cosmic humility that teaches us what it means to live surrounded by the love of God, moved along the river of that love, shaped by the current.

DAY 23

A Sword Will Pierce Your Own Soul

God, I brought him to the temple,
as you commanded each mother before me.
Forty days old, still-fresh body wrapped in cloth
around my soft middle. A day's journey
toward Jerusalem for the sake of surrender.

God, I missed home, missed my mom,
my friends. My breasts no longer ached,
my bleeding ceased, but still I wondered
how to return to the angel blaze
that left me light-soaked,
when I thought myself wise, certain of my role.
Magnify the Lord, rejoice in God.
But wonder wanes when sleep is shaped
by infant wakings, the child's shock
each time he stirs to find himself separate,
real now. My body, only his first source.
Oh, that tender dread rooted in my joy

at his entrance, my body's loss.
To know he will leave again and again until he's gone.

God, I grasp the cost. So when the old man's eyes
meet mine, his sacred knowing cleaves my soul,
as if to say I'm sorry this will hurt.
Still I unwrap the cloths, the baby's head
wobbling as I stretch him toward the stranger.
I surrender his body to the consecration.

God, I needed an angel to recognize
what Simeon saw through his own eyes:
Son of Man the prophets dreamed
now bare, anointed and lifted
toward the temple courts. Behold salvation.

God, *the glory of your people.*
He is blessed and my own soul unfurls
its scroll, images of this life:
late night feedings, whispered stories in the dark,
meat cut in bits, first knee scrape,
river splashes and laughter,
the songs I teach him as we clean.
The prophets' words I press into that boy's hands,
watch him stand in this place—
strength cloaked in peace,
his words cutting through the murmurs,
shouts of hosanna,
broken body.

God, you gave him to me
to nurture. I will give
again and again,
let that love pierce me.

DAY 24

Love That Nourishes

I love the Danish concept of *hygge*, which basically means coziness, meaningful connections, small pleasures, and gratitude during the coldest and darkest days of the year. A few years back, I read *The Little Book of Hygge: The Danish Way to Live Well.*[1] The book walks through all the principles of practicing hygge: delicious food, fires and candles, cozy socks, good friends and family under blankets, stories, games, togetherness.

If ever there is a time when Americans pause our productive lives long enough to practice hygge, it's this week. The days that lead up to Christmas, when the kids are out of school and we travel to be with family, when we bake treats, play nostalgic music, pull out the blankets, and watch feel-good movies—this is our hygge time!

For those of us who believe that the story of Christmas stretches wider than these days of celebration, who hold to a narrative that tells us God's cosmic humility offers an alternative way of joining the work of love, this week can carry something richer than feelings of togetherness or comfort. For us, Christmas can be nourishing.

As Augustine of Hippo, the fourth-century theologian, reminds us, "Placed in a manger, He became our food."[2] The one who was laid in a feeding trough will later call himself "the bread of life" (John 6:35), echoing his mother's song that celebrated a God who "fills the hungry with good things" (Luke 1:53). The one who took one boy's small meal of fish and bread, expanding it to feed the thousands (Matt. 14:13–21), is the same one who told his friends on his last night that his body was the bread they were eating (Matt. 26:26). This child we celebrate at Christmas grows up to call himself spiritual food. Food nourishes, strengthens, and comforts us.

So today, let's remember the nourishment of God as we practice hygge. I invite you to get up from your cozy spot on the couch (I see you!) and take some time to bake or make nourishing food. Perhaps you already have plans for that. The teachers need gifts and you're throwing together some cookies today, or the grandkids are arriving soon and you're making their favorite pumpkin bread. Maybe it's just you at home, but you know your neighbor would be delighted to receive some soup. Whether you are a natural cook or you never dirty a dish in your kitchen, let today be a moment when you create something nourishing for the sake of love. Love of yourself, love of your neighbor, love of your people. Love of God.

Here's a simple prayerful way to connect with God in the kitchen:

1. As you pull out each ingredient, thank God for the pleasure it brings to your life.
2. As you measure, pour, mix, or slice, consider the faces of each person who will eat this food. As their face comes to mind, offer a blessing on their behalf. Keep it easy! "Be close to _____," or "I hold _____ in your love."
3. As you pour the dough into the pan, or scoop the cookies onto the sheet, or watch your soup begin to bubble, picture yourself this Christmas. What will it look like for you to step into each family or friend gathering with a posture of love and a commitment to nourish those around you?
4. Put the pan into the oven or blend your soup. Close with a commitment to choose love over anxiety this week. To show up with a vision of transformative love that moves you and those around you to joy and goodness.

DAY 25

Love That Illumines

And there were shepherds living out in the fields nearby, keeping watch over their flocks at night. An angel of the Lord appeared to them, and the glory of the Lord shone around them, and they were terrified. But the angel said to them, "Do not be afraid. I bring you good news that will cause great joy for all the people. Today in the town of David a Savior has been born to you; he is the Messiah, the Lord. This will be a sign to you: You will find a baby wrapped in cloths and lying in a manger."

Suddenly a great company of the heavenly host appeared with the angel, praising God and saying,

> "Glory to God in the highest heaven,
> and on earth peace to those on whom his favor
> rests."

When the angels had left them and gone into heaven, the shepherds said to one another, "Let's go to Bethlehem and see this thing that has happened, which the Lord has told us about."

So they hurried off and found Mary and Joseph, and the baby, who was lying in the manger.

—Luke 2:8–16

One of the great gifts of the past five years of my life has been building and leading a youth ministry for the teenagers at my church. The young people I work with inhabit a world entirely unlike the one I knew as a teenager in the Texas Panhandle of the 1990s. Thirty years later, the kids I work with have been formed by the tiny computers buzzing in their pockets, a childhood interrupted by a terrifying pandemic, and the chaotic divisions of our country. They are growing up in New York City, among the most diverse cities in the world. Helping guide these young people through the turbulent teenage years, while supporting their spiritual growth, forces me to reframe and reimagine Christian faith for this generation of kids.

As my coleaders and I have worked to build this community of teens, we have established some well-loved traditions. We go away together a few times a year for retreats where everyone's phone is collected and kept by the leaders, allowing us all to look in each other's eyes, play games outside, hike, and have real conversations away from distractions. Our favorite tradition happens on the last night, when we sit around a fire for what we call story slam. There is something powerful and centering about sitting in a circle around a fire in a quiet place. It's an experience rare yet so essential for these city kids. Community around fire has been a ritual for most of human history. When we circle around a fire together, we tap into connection, warmth, a spark of recognition in our consciousness of meaning that's bigger than our daily physical needs. During story slam, we share stories about the themes we've explored that weekend. What have we discovered? Who do we want to be? What matters in our lives?

Circling around a fire has an ancient grounding effect for most of us. The presence of contained flames can help calm our nervous systems and allow us to focus on one another. And often, we find ourselves telling stories, laughing, and connecting. That's not by accident. Our bodies know that to be around a fire is to be nourished, protected, and welcomed.

"The people who walked in darkness have seen a great light," the prophet wrote. "Those who lived in a land of deep darkness—on them light has shined" (Isa. 9:2 NRSVue). This is a prophecy of the coming Christ, one we often hear read aloud on Christmas Eve. The people have lived with a veil of darkness, fumbling through their lives, longing for something more; but revelation is coming, and it will allow their eyes to finally make sense of the reality that's been there all along. Later in Isaiah, the prophet speaks to those who have encountered that light, for whom the Messiah has arrived: "Arise, shine; for your light has come, and the glory of the Lord has risen upon you" (60:1 NRSVue). Those of us who have heard these words read over and over from the pulpit may forget to notice the power of this idea. Who is shining? It's the people who walked in darkness. They have not only encountered the light; it has risen upon them, like the rosy softness of a sunrise, coating their faces in gold. In this passage, it's not simply that they can now see; it's that they *glow*, reflecting light to those they face.

With this kind of prophetic text in the hearts and minds of the Hebrew people, it's not a surprise that the story of Jesus's birth would involve radiant light shocking the darkness, inviting the people in the story to a luminous transformation. A child is born, and the star shines in the middle of the night. The angels arrive and astonish the shepherds snoozing on the mountain. The night sky bursts open. Despite all the technological transformations of the last half century and the deep divisions among Christians—political, theological, and otherwise—most churches the world over will continue the tradition of lighting candles this Christmas Eve, passing the flame from one wick to another. The ritual of light in the darkness, flame's ability to grow as it is transferred, never being depleted in the sharing—these are the symbols of the love that arrives through God's cosmic humility, God's self-giving love in the form of a human.

As the Gospel writer John says in his own creative take on the nativity, "In him was life, and the life was the light of all people. The light shines in the darkness, and the darkness did not overtake it" (1:4–5 NRSVue). When I teach my students about light, I often repeat a story I heard years ago describing the joy of playing outside as a kid on a summer night, how the dusk settles and the glow from our home's window calls us inside. I ask them, "When you open the screen door, running into your bright, lit up house, does your mom yell, 'Honey, please don't let the darkness in!'? Never."[1] We all understand this. Darkness cannot sneak in when light is present. Light always pushes back darkness, not the other way around.

When we say that light illuminates the truth, that's what we mean. Light reveals what's there, and if light is present, darkness must flee. There is a twofold nature to the image of light in Scripture, which often shows up in the form of flame. Fire not only warms and illuminates but also transforms wood into ash, burning anything in its path. In the story of the birth of Jesus, the shepherds are warmed, but Herod is threatened. "Fire is essential for life and civilization, and fire is a threat to both."[2]

When our students and leaders gather around the fire, our faces lit in the flickering ember, we see each other in a new way. The blue light of our phones is a poor imitation of fire's golden incandescence, carbon particles kindled to glow, then releasing into the night air. The copper brilliance of fire itself is a chemical reaction, but we experience it as a source of light and heat. For us it plays the role of revealing what we couldn't have seen in the darkness.

Fire is one of the gifts in the telling of Jesus's birth: We see flame throughout the story: a brilliant star in the sky guiding the shepherds and the wise scholars from the east, a band of illuminated angels singing, Joseph receiving revelations of truth in the middle of the night. All throughout the story, darkness is replaced by clarity, revealing a God who, motivated by love, comes to us as a great light. The arrival of Jesus offers a new way of seeing, not only to the participants in the story but also to all of us seeking that light two millennia later. "I am the light of the world," Jesus would teach (John 8:12). Light transforms the sky, but it also transforms our inner selves.

We humans have always sought meaning, explanation for the pain and beauty of the world. We can often experience our existential angst alone, feeling as if we're trapped in our own interior lives, struggling to see our place in the human story. But every once in a while, we get moments of communal clarity. When we gather around a fire with people we love, allowing ourselves to be loved in return and reminded of our place in the community, the big questions of life may no longer carry the dread of anxiety. In the light of community, even our uncertainty can orient us within a greater mystery, holding us steady. Light can do that for us because its very nature is to reveal.

In her novel *Gilead*, Marilynne Robinson reflects on those moments of radiant transformation, in which we see the reality of God in the world: "It has seemed to me sometimes as though the Lord breathes on this poor gray ember of Creation and it turns to radiance—for a moment or a year or the span of a life. And then it sinks back into itself again, and to look at it no one would know it had anything to do with fire, or light." It can be difficult to hold onto these moments of radiance. The world returns to seeming ordinary again. We go back to dishes and errands and gray winter afternoons. Yet Robinson suggests that perhaps the light hasn't vanished after all. Perhaps we have simply forgotten how to notice. "Wherever you turn your eyes the world can shine like transfiguration," Robinson concludes. "You don't have to bring a thing to it except a little willingness to see."[3]

That willingness to see is the necessary entry point to what Richard Beck calls enchantment: "A holy capacity to see and experience God in the world."[4] He calls it bumping into God, which no doubt is what the shepherds experienced when the luminous angels hovered in the inky night above them.[5] What allowed them the holy capacity to see? What gave Mary the wonder she carried and the words she sang? Beck says we cultivate that vision through spiritual practice, especially through contemplation. "Relationship with God," he writes, "is more seeing than believing."[6] In other words, in the story of Christ's birth, the shepherds and Mary aren't asked to sign off on a correct statement of faith to encounter the glory of the divine. The flame came first, and they paid attention. Their light had come, and they allowed the glory of the Lord to rise upon them. Their revelation came before any certainty.

Where are you being invited to see, to pay attention to the light this Christmas? If we believe the presence of the divine is all around us in the most mundane, ordinary spaces of our lives, we have every possibility of bumping into the light of God. And that light, like the candles we will light across our sanctuaries in just a few days, doesn't deplete as the light is shared. There is always more flame, always more love to behold.

DAY 26

Here I Am, Spirit

In the Day 25 entry, we explored what Richard Beck calls "bumping into God." Beck teaches that our capacity to experience God's nearness is something we can cultivate through habit, practice, and formation.[1]

As we celebrate the embodiment of the God who is love, let's consider the habits we might nurture as we learn to pay attention to the light around us, remembering that the flame doesn't deplete as it is shared. Today, can we come to prayer willing to pay attention like the shepherds, amazed by the illuminated hillside and the story of God come to us? Let's attend to the world around us in case we "bump into God," finding comfort in a Creator who is always close, who wants us to know that we are loved and wanted and welcome.

This is a practice you can do every day, especially in this season when it's most likely dark when you wake in the morning and often dark when you get home from work or school. As with other practices in this book, this one asks you to choose a word or phrase you would like to focus on. Maybe you want to use this word now and throughout the weeks following Christmas Day as a reminder of the light and love found in God's cosmic humility. Or maybe you find yourself drawn to one word today and a different word tomorrow. Either option is okay.

If you don't know where to start, it might help to make a list of what you imagine this season of Christmas—the twelve days the church invites us to celebrate—will cultivate in you. When you reach January 6, what do you hope your practices around Advent and Christmas will have nurtured inside you: Belief? Wonder? Curiosity? Delight?

Once you've picked a word, find a cozy spot and light a candle. Sit still and welcome the Holy Spirit to join you here. You can pray something like this:

Breathe in: *Here I am, Spirit.*
Breathe out: *Here you are, Spirit.*

Set a timer for five minutes. As you sit in silence, imagine holding your chosen word in your heart. Whenever your mind wanders, bring it back with gentleness to the word you've chosen. You may want to close with a prayer like this one, adapted from Marilynne Robinson's novel *Gilead*:

God, who comes as light and love, may everywhere I turn reveal a world that shines like transfiguration. Give me willingness to see. Amen.

CHRISTMAS EVE

Love as a Laboring Woman

So Joseph also went up from the town of Nazareth in Galilee to Judea, to Bethlehem the town of David, because he belonged to the house and line of David. He went there to register with Mary, who was pledged to be married to him and was expecting a child. While they were there, the time came for the baby to be born, and she gave birth to her firstborn, a son. She wrapped him in cloths and placed him in a manger, because there was no guest room available for them.

—Luke 2:4–7

For a long time I have kept silent,
    I have been quiet and held myself back.
But now, like a woman in childbirth,
    I cry out, I gasp and pant.

—Isaiah 42:14

When I was pregnant with my firstborn, I was twenty-eight years old and terrified. And, book nerd that I am, I did what I've always done when gripped with fear: I took a class. This class was called hypnobirthing. It's a theory of childbirth that a woman in labor can rise above pain through entering and remaining in a state of meditation throughout the birthing process. To prepare, I listened to meditation practices on my iPod (this was 2008) before bed each night. I practiced deep breathing exercises. And mostly, I worked hard to convince myself that my experience of childbirth could be something closer to peace than pain.[1]

Listen, readers, some people are truly capable of meditating to the point of deep contentment during labor. They are superheroes. Also, I'm pretty sure these people only exist in Norway. The rest of us have a choice: We can breathe or we can fight our bodies. Either way, the baby is coming.

After giving birth three times—and each delivery somehow matching the personality of each child (this is true and I don't know how to explain it)—I have learned this: In the chaos of giving birth, the body takes over. No matter how much gentle music played in the hospital room or how many times I prayerfully considered the beauty of my coming child, my body always told my brain and feelings to shut down. She was in charge now. Once the thinking mind goes quiet, the birthing magic can really begin. At that point there is no longer the prayer of the mind, no longer the prayer of the emotions. There is only the panting prayer of the body.

Once my body told the rest of me who was in charge, I could no longer control the meditative process. I could only be the body God made me to be, a body that groaned in the way my birthing ancestors have groaned since the beginning. In the most intense stage of childbirth, a laboring person must come to a moment of acceptance, relaxing the birthing muscles despite a natural inclination to clench and tighten. This is paradoxical work, transformation that requires more than deep breathing. It requires *groaning*. A study in 2022 found that vocalizing during the birthing process doesn't just allow the mother to work with her body to bring the child into the world, it actually protects the body during birth.[2]

Another study showed that laboring women who scream or cry are more likely to experience increased anxiety during birth, making delivery even more difficult and painful.[3] There is a powerful distinction in these studies between the deep groaning that brings the body into focus and helps calm the muscles required for birth and the screaming that tightens the same muscles. One sound is the song of the whale in the water, deep and warm and life-giving. One is the sound of fear.

I like to consider a groaning, birthing mother when I imagine Paul's powerful description of the Holy Spirit in Romans. When we are weak, Paul writes, the Holy Spirit steps in and helps us. The Spirit doesn't show up with anxiety-inducing rules that make us feel worse about our weaknesses. We don't get a serious parental conversation. There's no yelling or crying. Only groans. As in childbirth, groaning is our way through the challenges of our own limits. When we don't know what to pray, the Spirit groans on our behalf (Rom. 8:26). And the Spirit not only groans on our behalf but also joins all of creation in groaning for the work of God to be completed in this world (8:20–22).

These last few days before Christmas, I invite us to imagine the God who not only takes on the body of a human child but is described by the writer of Isaiah as actively birthing a new and beautiful story into the world. In this story of all things being made new, God is both the one giving birth and the one being ushered into the world as savior (Rev. 21:5). Always at the same time.

These verses in Isaiah where God is imagined as a laboring mother were written when the people of Israel had been forced from their homes and taken to Babylon. In the verses before this, God speaks comfort to them.[4] The Lord announces to the people that while "the former things have taken place," something new is coming and it will "spring into being" (42:9). The writer moves into song, praising God. Then God responds:

> For a long time I have held my peace;
>   I have kept still and restrained myself;
> now I will cry out like a woman in labor;
>   I will gasp and pant. (42:14 NRSVue)

The Hebrew word Isaiah uses for gasp is *pa'ah,* best translated as "bellow."[5] It's an animal sound. Here, God replies to the praise of the people by becoming wild with love. What makes the divine lose restraint to the point of making animal noises? Love of God's own people, the same sort of love that causes a perfectly respectable lady to groan while nude on a birthing ball. Labor brings out the wild creature in us. God wants us to know that the wild creature is there within the divine as well. In the groaning of the Spirit on our behalf, in the hope of something new after the devastation of exile, in the creation of a new world where justice is served and flourishing is possible, we see this: The Lord is our birthing mother. With groans and power, the Holy One who loves us, who is the embodiment of love, is actively moving that beauty into the world.

With that in mind, we find ourselves on Christmas Eve. Our reading has brought us to Mary and Joseph, forced to travel from Nazareth to Bethlehem, ninety miles on foot through the Judean hills with Mary nearing the end of her pregnancy. After what is most likely a journey of ten to fourteen days, Mary is forced to give birth in a place she doesn't know, among people she doesn't know.

When I was pregnant with my youngest, knowing how well I did with hypnobirthing (not the best) with my first birth and how disconnected I felt from my body when I was pumped up with an epidural the second time I birthed, I longed for something between. I didn't need to be the hero of my own birthing story, meditating myself into bliss, but I also wanted to actively participate in the process. So I hired Jen, a doula with a no-nonsense belief in me and my baby and a willingness to bring me back from the abyss when I began to let fear and anxiety gain control. Jen and I had several months to get to know each other ahead of time. She joined my laboring at home, coaching my husband in how to support me, and got us to the hospital exactly on time. By then, I knew I'd found the secret to enduring the pain of labor: being cared for, being loved, being touched and cheered on and believed in. I hold that final birth as a sacred touchstone of what is possible, not because I'm a badass but because the woman who believed in my badassery also helped me believe it about myself. It was Jen who gave me permission to groan and bellow and whale song my way through that birth.

I hope Mary had a Jen. I hope there was a midwife in the neighborhood who saw Mary's state and showed up to help. I hope that, whatever the traditional Christmas descriptions say about Mary's lack of a comfy room to birth in, someone was there supplying fresh hay and blankets, water and encouragement to move her body, to embrace the sounds of the animals nearby.

We know what love is. It is a mother birthing in a strange place, not because she wants to but because she bravely said yes. We know what love is. It is a divine Creator welcoming home the creation that had been taken away. We know what love is. It is the cosmic humility of a God who both groans in labor pains and chooses to enter the world through birth—blood and mucus and that first desperate breath.

Today, as you light your candle and sing of a "Silent Night," may you remember that Christmas did not arrive in silence. It came through the cries of labor, the groans of a mother, and the first desperate breath of a newborn God teaching us what love looks like.

CHRISTMAS DAY

Mary Says Yes

Listen. In the coral kitchen:
the sound of a purring gas stove
and the cat splashing across the linoleum
after a brown rubber band.
And in the distance the noon church bells
chime song after song announcing the angel

who always appears at lunchtime,
a voice like rivers. We've been here
before I say but can't help the smile.
By now friends in this sacred multiverse,
over and over salvation coming.
Do I want to be cosmic queen, mother
of weepers, the people's saint of petitions,
raise this child for love?

Oh for love. Will I patch his corduroy
knees, chase his wild laughter,
concern myself with his awkward claims

and holy mysteries, until I lie facedown
on this linoleum, thirty-three years in,
grief the sword that eventually pierces us all?
I offer the angel a cookie. He asks for milk.
Even now in this time and land, I remember
my son taken by the ones who crush us.

Listen, I know about death,
I say to the crumb-mouthed mystic wanderer,
this blinking bewildered gaze of God.
Here—then all cloud, blue-pink sky.
Who wasn't made for this? Hope and life, loss
and life again. But listen: The angel flows
away and I hear my soul's long harmony,
the gas stove lit like the Lord expanding
everything, creating space to hold us.

Acknowledgments

It's been such a delight to work with the entire team at Brazos on this book as well as *Blessed Are the Rest of Us*. Katelyn Beaty, it is a true gift to know that my editor gets what I'm trying to do. Thank you for sharpening my work in all the best ways. Paula Gibson, thank you for your beautiful vision for book design. I'm so delighted you went with my dream of an original illustration and worked with me to make it happen. All my gratitude to Mayuko Fujino for creating our magical Mary on the cover. And, of course, thanks to Erin Smith in marketing, and Julie Zahm, Tammy Ditmore, Melinda Timmer, and all the behind-the-scenes hands at Brazos who had a hand in the editing. My agent Zoë Pagnamenta always makes time for me, remembers to ask the questions I miss, and believes in my work. I'm grateful.

When I first started writing poetry in college, I shared all my poems with my bestie Molly, who made me belly laugh daily, loved words, and gave me excellent feedback. Twenty-five years later, Molly Hunt read every one of these poems (and more). Her presence in my life and help in choosing what to include here were a true gift. (John, I know you helped too.)

I had the eyes of several other folks as well, particularly friends who gave me feedback for how to make my poetry accessible to all readers, especially those who don't consider themselves "poetry people." Big thanks especially to Margo Pumar, Heather Avis, Erin Lane, and Jayne Sugg. Nancy Filkin, who has been a mentor in my life, cheered on all these poems, especially the ones that looked very different fifteen years ago. Nancy, your belief in my work means the world.

I'm grateful to Cara Meredith and Amy Julia Becker for their constant support of my writing, willingness to look at drafts, and consistent wisdom. Thanks to my brother, Jason Boyett, for being my go-to for opinions on design and for always making time for me.

Thanks to Stephanie Ricke, who generously opened her beautiful apartment to me so I could have some quiet space for writing. Also, Izzy Zarra, your feedback with illustrations was super helpful. I adore my coleaders in the youth ministry at Good Shepherd New York. Big thanks to Tim Ronco and Melanie Thompson for helping me with this subtitle. And of course, to Austin Applebach, who wasn't in the van when we had that conversation but would have been helpful, I'm sure!

And to my guys—August, Brooks, and Ace—you have watched me pray, try to pray, read, quit reading and scroll my phone instead, drink coffee as a prayer, journal as a prayer, and sometimes just hug you as a prayer. You all know how much I long for wonder and stillness and how my faith is as wobbly as the next person's. Your lives have been my greatest teachers in the unhurried life. Let's go put up the Christmas tree. I need to weep at your tiny baby faces on those ornaments.

And Chris, you are part of every book I write. Thanks for sharing your brilliant mind with me and making space to think with me through all my ideas. It's a gift to trust a man who allows himself to be shaped by the virtues of Jesus. Your faith is a joy to me and to our family.

And finally, Mom, whose life has taught me that early mornings are for drinking coffee in the dim light, reading, and praying. This one's for you.

Notes

Introduction Slowing Down to Savor the Mystery

1. Annie Dillard, *The Writing Life* (Harper & Row, 1989), 32.

2. Ruth Haley Barton, "Make a Joyful Silence," *Sojourners* 38, no. 2 (February 2009): 32.

3. Martha C. Nussbaum, *The Fragility of Goodness: Luck and Ethics in Greek Tragedy and Philosophy* (Cambridge University Press, 2001), 302–3.

4. Nussbaum, *Fragility of Goodness*, 10–12.

5. Mark Scandrette, *The Ninefold Path of Jesus: Hidden Wisdom of the Beatitudes* (InterVarsity, 2021), 10.

How to Read a Poem Prayerfully

1. Kimberly Mills, host, *Speaking of Psychology*, podcast, episode 225, "Why Our Attention Spans Are Shrinking, with Gloria Mark, PhD," American Psychological Association, February 2023, https://www.apa.org/news/podcasts/speaking-of-psychology/attention-spans.

Day 1 Hope Begins with Looking Up

1. I owe this reference to my pastor Michael Rudzena, who made this point and introduced me to Weil's work.

2. Simone Weil, *Waiting for God*, trans. Emma Craufurd (Harper Perennial Modern Classics, 2009), 127.

3. Weil, *Waiting for God*, 127.

4. Weil, *Waiting for God*, 127.

5. Michael Rudzena, sermon, posted November 28, 2021, by Good Shepherd, New York, YouTube, https://www.youtube.com/watch?v=4rbRSGSg55k.

Day 5 Hope Begins with *Yes*

1. Kelley Nikondeha, *The First Advent in Palestine: Reversals, Resistance, and the Ongoing Complexity of Hope* (Broadleaf, 2022), 74.

2. Nikondeha, *First Advent in Palestine*, 79.

3. Kate Bowler, "On Being in a Body," interview by Krista Tippett, *On Being*, podcast, September 21, 2023, MP3/audio, https://onbeing.org/programs/kate-bowler-on-being-in-a-body/.

4. I owe these broader ideas to Kelley Nikondeha and her work in *First Advent in Palestine*.

5. Nikondeha, *First Advent in Palestine*, 84–93.

Day 7 See My Pockets, Lord

1. Roger Robinson, "A Portable Paradise," *On Being* with Krista Tippett, November 2, 2020, https://onbeing.org/poetry/a-portable-paradise/.

Day 8 The Blessing of Completeness

1. Walter Brueggemann, *Peace: Living Toward a Vision* (Chalice, 2001), 15.

2. Shout-out to my sister-in-law Aimee, organizer of the pills, doctor's office notetaker, and queen of understanding paperwork!

Day 10 *Lectio Divina*

1. Pope Benedict XVI, transcript, "*General Audience, St. Peter's Square, Wednesday, 2 May 2007: Origen of Alexandria: The Thought (2)*," The Holy See, Benedict XVI, Audiences, May 2, 2007, https://www.vatican.va

/content/benedict-xvi/en/audiences/2007/documents/hf_ben-xvi_aud_20070502.html.

Day 11 The Slow Work of Peace

1. Madeleine L'Engle, "First Coming," in *The Ordering of Love: The New and Collected Poems of Madeleine L'Engle* (Shaw Books, 2005), 242.

2. Gerard Manley Hopkins, "Peace," in *Poems of Gerard Manley Hopkins*, ed. Robert Bridges (Oxford University Press, 1918), 39.

3. Taylor Swift, "Bad Blood," track 4 on *1989*, Republic Records, 2014.

Day 13 Peace Nourished by Loss

1. Walter Brueggemann, *Isaiah 1–39*, Westminster Bible Companion (Westminster John Knox, 1998), 97–98.

2. Lore Ferguson Wilbert, *The Understory* (Brazos, 2024), especially her reflections on old-growth forest soil and nutrient inheritance in part 2 ("Forest Litter," "Soil") and part 3 ("Mycelia," "Forest").

3. Wilbert, *Understory*, 49.

Day 14 Peace as Pronouncing Blessing

1. Barbara Brown Taylor, *An Altar in the World: A Geography of Faith* (HarperOne, 2009), 187–201.

Day 15 Building Our Capacity for Joy

1. I tell this story more fully in my book *Blessed Are the Rest of Us: How Limits and Longing Make Us Whole* (Brazos, 2024).

2. Wendell Berry, "Manifesto: The Mad Farmer Liberation Front," in *The Selected Poems of Wendell Berry* (Counterpoint, 1998), 87.

3. "How Many Babies Are Born a Year?," United Nations, Department of Economic and Social Affairs, Population Division, 2024, accessed November 29, 2025, https://data.unicef.org/how-many/how-many-babies-are-born-a-year/.

4. Michael Rudzena, sermon, posted December 15, 2024, by Good Shepherd, New York, YouTube, https://www.youtube.com/watch?v=tWa_KQubm9A.

Day 18 The Opposite of Anxiety

1. In the mid-twentieth century, psychiatrist Dr. Murray Bowen developed family systems theory, which he used to explore the emotional and generational dynamics of families. He particularly theorized regarding how anxiety travels through a group as explored by Ilene Strauss Cohen, "Understanding Bowen Family Systems Theory," *Psychology Today*, November 13, 2023, https://www.psychologytoday.com/us/blog/your-emotional-meter/202311/understanding-bowen-family-systems-theory. But it wasn't until the 1980s that Dr. Edwin H. Friedman examined Bowen's ideas in *Generation to Generation: Family Process in Church and Synagogue* (Guilford Press, 1985) and coined the term "nonanxious presence."

2. Kate Bowler, host, *Everything Happens with Kate Bowler*, podcast, "Father Greg Boyle: Unshakable Goodness," October 8, 2024, https://katebowler.com/podcasts/unshakable-goodness/.

3. Bowler, "Father Greg Boyle: Unshakable Goodness."

4. Walter Brueggemann, *Isaiah 1–39*, Westminster Bible Companion (Westminster John Knox, 1998), 114.

5. Bowler, "Freedom of Loving and Being Loved."

Day 19 Releasing Ego, Embracing Joy

1. I first discovered the phrase "the dream of God" as another way of referring to "the kingdom of God" in the work of Stephanie Spellers, particularly her book *The Church Cracked Open: Disruption, Decline, and New Hope for Beloved Community* (Church Publishing, 2021). I explore her ideas more fully in my book: *Blessed Are the Rest of Us: How Limits and Longing Make Us Whole* (Brazos, 2024).

2. Richard Rohr, *Breathing Under Water: Spirituality and the Twelve Steps* (SPCK, 2016), 22.

3. Rohr, *Breathing Under Water*, 22.

Day 20 How to Bear Sorrow

1. Etty Hillesum, *An Interrupted Life: The Diaries, 1941–1943 and Letters from Westerbork*, trans. Arnold J. Pomerans (Henry Holt, 1996), 96.
2. Hillesum, *Interrupted Life*, 96.

Day 22 Love Is the Container; Love Is the Story

1. Stanley Hauerwas, "Stanley Hauerwas: Love, Suffering, and Theology (Full Interview)," interview by Evan Rosa, *The Table Video*, Biola University Center for Christian Thought, May 27, 2017, https://cct.biola.edu/love-suffering-theology/.
2. Hauerwas, "Love, Suffering, and Theology."
3. Hauerwas, "Love, Suffering, and Theology."
4. Iris Murdoch, "The Sublime and the Good," in *Existentialists and Mystics: Writings on Philosophy and Literature*, ed. Peter J. Conradi (Penguin, 1999), 348.
5. Murdoch, "Sublime and the Good," 348.

Day 24 Love That Nourishes

1. Meik Wiking, *The Little Book of Hygge: The Danish Way to Live Well* (Penguin UK, 2016).
2. Augustine, *Sermons for Christmas and Epiphany*, trans. Thomas Comerford Lawler, Ancient Christian Writers, vol. 15 (Newman, 1952), 96.

Day 25 Love That Illumines

1. I have no notes for this illustration, but my memory tells me I first heard this from Matt Chandler in Abilene, Texas, at the Grace gathering, circa 1997–1999. It stuck with me.
2. Lauren F. Winner, *Wearing God: Clothing, Laughter, Fire, and Other Overlooked Ways of Meeting God* (HarperOne, 2015), 206.
3. Marilynne Robinson, *Gilead* (Farrar, Straus & Giroux, 2004), 245.
4. Richard Beck, *Hunting Magic Eels: Recovering an Enchanted Faith in a Skeptical Age* (Broadleaf Books, 2021), 5–6.
5. Beck, *Hunting Magic Eels*, 9.

6. Richard Beck, "Seeing God," *Experimental Theology with Richard Beck* (Substack), June 12, 2023, accessed December 1, 2025, https://richardbeck.substack.com/p/seeing-god.

Day 26 Here I Am, Spirit

1. Richard Beck, "Seeing God," *Experimental Theology with Richard Beck* (Substack), June 12, 2023, accessed December 1, 2025, https://richardbeck.substack.com/p/seeing-god.

Christmas Eve Love as a Laboring Woman

1. Also, I wore a button on my coat that said, "Only happy birth stories, please! My baby is listening."
2. Joana Nunes Neta, Melania Maria Amorim, Julianna Guendler, Alexandre Delgado, Andréa Lemos, and Leila Katz, "Vocalization During the Second Stage of Labor to Prevent Perineal Trauma: A Randomized Controlled Trial," *European Journal of Obstetrics, Gynecology, and Reproductive Biology* 275 (2022): 46–53, https://doi.org/10.1016/j.ejogrb.2022.06.007.
3. Bibi Marziyeh Hashemi Asl, Atiyeh Vatanchi, Nahid Golmakani, and Alireza Najafi, "Relationship Between Behavioral Indices of Pain During Labor Pain with Pain Intensity and Duration of Delivery," *Electronic Physician* 10, no. 1 (2018): 6240–48, https://doi.org/10.19082/6240.
4. The foundation of this essay is based on Lauren Winner's wonderful book *Wearing God: Clothing, Laughter, Fire, and Other Overlooked Ways of Meeting God* (HarperOne, 2015). Her chapter "Laboring Woman" gave me the framework of the themes explored here, particularly this understanding of Isaiah 42. Winner, *Wearing God*, 136.
5. Winner, *Wearing God*, 138–39.

Micha Boyett (MFA, Syracuse University) is the author of *Blessed Are the Rest of Us* and *Found: A Story of Questions, Grace, and Everyday Prayer*. She is also a contributor to the *New York Times* bestseller *A Rhythm of Prayer*. Her writing on prayer, disability, and the grace of ordinary life has appeared in publications including *The Washington Post* and *Christianity Today*. Boyett cohosts *The Lucky Few* podcast and is the creator of *The Slow Way* podcast and newsletter. She lives with her husband and three children in northern New Jersey.

Connect with Micha

www.michaboyett.com

@michaboyett; @acefaceismyfriend; @theluckyfewpod

michaboyett

michaboyett.substack.com